Declutter Your Home:

Simple Step-by-Step Home Decluttering Strategies on How to Declutter and Organize to De-Stress and Simplify Your Life

Madeline Crawford

© **Copyright 2019 by Madeline Crawford - All rights reserved.**

The contents of this book may not be reproduced, duplicated, or transmitted without direct written permission from the author.

Under no circumstances will any legal responsibility or blame be held against the publisher for any reparation, damages, or monetary loss due to the information herein, either directly or indirectly.

Legal Notice:

This book is copyright protected; it is only for personal use. You cannot amend, distribute, sell, use, quote, or paraphrase any part of the content within this book without the consent of the author.

Disclaimer Notice:

Please note the information contained within this document is for educational and entertainment purposes only. Every attempt has been made to provide accurate, up to date, and completely reliable information. No warranties of any kind are expressed or implied. Readers acknowledge that the author is not engaging in the rendering of legal, financial, medical, or professional advice. The content of this book has been derived from various sources. Please consult a licensed professional before attempting any techniques outlined in this book.

By reading this document, the reader agrees that under no circumstances is the author responsible for any losses, direct or indirect, which are incurred as a result of the use of the information contained within this document, including, but not limited to, —errors, omissions, or inaccuracies.

Table of Contents

Introduction:

Chapter 1: "My House is a Mess!" (The Home Clutter Problem)

Chapter 2: The Proper Mindset for Decluttering Success

Chapter 3: Overview of the Decluttering Process

Chapter 4: Living Room and Family Room

Chapter 5: Bedrooms

Chapter 6: Kitchen

Chapter 7: Bathrooms and Laundry Room

Chapter 8: Closets

Chapter 9: Storage Room

Chapter 10: Entryways, Mudrooms, and Foyers

Chapter 11: Home Office

Chapter 12: Basement and Attic

Chapter 13: Books and Paper Documents

Chapter 14: Garage

Chapter 15: Dealing with Items You Love

Chapter 16: Decluttering in One Day

Bonus Chapter: Decluttering Before Moving

Conclusion

References

Introduction:

If you have a countertop in your kitchen housing various appliances that you haven't used for months, a pile of mail on the table in your home office, or floor areas that require a lot of skill to navigate through, then you have a problem. Specifically, a clutter problem. Understanding that you have this problem in your home must be the reason why you have picked this book.

Here are some facts concerning the clutter problem:

- According to a study by the Soap and Detergent Association, getting rid of an estimated 40% of the housework required for an average family is possible by removing clutter.
- About 23% of adults are late on their bill payments and are forced to settle the late payment fees due to disorganization according to a study by Harris Interactive.
- A survey of 1,000 American women by OnePoll shows that 10% of these women

experience a feeling of depression anytime they open their closets.
- A LexisNexis study shows that, of the numerous items we own, only 20% of them are put to use.
- A Huffington Post survey indicates that clutter-related worry ranks as the 5th highest trigger for stress in Americans.

To solve the problem of clutter, this book takes a look at the various aspects of clutter and how to go about decluttering. The decluttering process focuses on the different rooms in the home and gives detailed steps on how to declutter each room. You learn how to develop a decluttering mindset which is crucial in achieving your decluttering goals.

As a mother, my house was once a cluttered mess. Clutter in my home kept increasing, not because I wasn't doing my best to organize the home, but because I kept making new purchases without getting rid of the old items. From my perspective, I didn't believe I was doing anything wrong until I enlisted the help of a professional for a day. Within a week, I saw drastic changes in the appearance of my home.

To make progress and achieved the home I desired, I kept doing a lot of research into different decluttering ideas in order to come up with the most effective solution. Through my years spent gaining knowledge and my experience decluttering my home, I have found out a lot about decluttering, from the importance of small wins in decluttering to the KonMari strategy, and many more.

My passion for writing this book is to help individuals, especially mothers, who are in a similar spot as I was a few years ago. As a mother, clutter in your home is not an indication of laziness or lack of effort; it just means it is time to find something that will guide you onto the right path.

There are numerous reasons why decluttering is important. Your home is a reflection of who you are. It is a space in which you should feel safe and comfortable, creating a strategy for the future as well as being productive.

Ensuring that the home is clutter-free allows you to enhance your productivity. It also has health benefits as it provides freedom from stress and anxiety.

Here are the replies from individuals that have applied various decluttering strategies to improve their home and their life:

"My life had been a mess after the loss of my mother. I was keeping all her possessions in the hopes that I would find relief from my grief. In the end, I was doing myself more harm than good. Every time I looked at one of her dresses or shoes, I would instantly remember that I couldn't see her anymore.

The break I desired came in the form of methods to declutter items of sentimental value. I wasn't finding it easy, but I took a step to make digital copies of the possessions that mattered most to me. To ease the process of letting go, I called a friend I knew was into charitable deeds. I had him clear out the storage while I watched. With the items gone, I have no regrets. I simply scroll through my photo gallery anytime I want to recall some memories of the woman I hold dear in my heart." – Jenn

"The idea of decluttering wasn't new to me, but I thought I wasn't making any form of reasonable progress. I searched for a lot of information on how to get through this slump. Of all the articles and books I read, the information that helped me the most was focusing on small wins.

My initial focus was on clutter in the entire home. I hadn't taken time to look at my progress in the rooms I had decluttered. I am a lot more motivated to take an extra step now more than ever." – James, NY

This book will provide all the steps you require to declutter each space in your home effectively. You will also find information regarding the importance of the small wins strategy in becoming an expert on the one-day decluttering process.

Solving the problem of clutter in the home is vital so that you can avoid the many issues associated with excessive clutter. Some common problems include injury from tripping over items and stepping on toys in addition to the embarrassment it causes anytime you have a visitor. Health problems associated with increased clutter in the home also include stress and depression. These are some of the critical things that decluttering can help you avoid.

Why You Should Get This Book

The strategies you are about to read can be implemented by anyone regardless of your profession, age, or amount of time available. There are practical actions that you can do as soon as you complete a chapter to get instant results before you even reach the end of the book. In addition to improving your life through decluttering, this book also gives you many excellent tips to help you along the way.

Chapter 1: "My House is a Mess!" (The Home Clutter Problem)

Chapter 1: "My House is a Mess!" (The Home Clutter Problem)

I was finally done with what I would tag as the worst day of my work life.

Frustrated and angry, I kept replaying the early hours of the day in my head. How did I end up leaving my work documents at home? Why did I have my utility bills and a copy of my tax returns in my bag? These were the thoughts that kept bothering me.

I brushed these thoughts aside as soon as my house came into view. My focus now was on finding my work documents. That was more important at the moment, or so I thought.

On opening the door and stepping into the house, I was greeted by the answer to my questions. My home was a mess. There were large piles of clutter lying around. I hadn't created time to put the house in order for a while.

I had my answer, but where did I put my documents? I kept trying to recall where I placed the documents, but every room I thought of had the same appearance of a cluttered mess. My stress was steadily building. The one place

I hoped to find comfort and peace had the exact opposite effect on my life.

During the search for my documents, moving from one room to the other, I tripped and fell over a stack of books on the floor. I was in a rush, so I didn't take notes. Nonetheless, this was the last straw.

My journey towards making my home a clutter-free zone didn't occur in one night. It was a process that I had to repeat over a few months until I achieved the initial results. The later stages involved actively ensuring that I didn't go back to having clutter around the home.

So, how do you define clutter and decluttering?

Simple, clutter is any object, item, or possession that doesn't offer any useful function despite occupying storage space within the home. In most cases, clutter is often a result of indecision on your part as an individual. It appears in the form of your inability to decide on the right place to keep particular objects, what objects to discard, and which things matter the most to us.

Decluttering, on the other hand, is an action you take in which you rid your home of the clutter that you have accumulated over the past days, months, or years. It involves making tough decisions that can help improve your life and create a permanent turnaround in your home.

The increase in the amount of clutter in the home is not a recent development. It is an increase that has been making steady progress from as far back as the Industrial Revolution. The Industrial Revolution was a turning point in history, which gave rise to the development of factories due to the economic freedom and technological advancements of the time.

Factories provided an opportunity to engage in mass production of different products. This increase in the production of goods led to a drop in the prices of these products. The ultimate outcome was a lifestyle of consumerism in which individuals had the opportunity to buy numerous products with each having unique features, all affordable with the salaries that they earned.

The promotion of socialist values that drove the increase in wealth of the middle class as well as the outsourcing of production processes further resulted in a reduction in the price of goods, making them even more affordable. Thus, people adopted the consumerist lifestyle with open arms.

The effects of this lifestyle remain noticeable in today's society where companies are spending large sums of money on marketing campaigns and adverts to promote the purchase of products. The boost in the number of products being released also means that people keep looking to make the latest purchase of the latest products.

Since consumers usually want to keep up with the latest advancements in technology to avoid being left out, it is easy to find homes filled with clothes, electronics, and other items in good condition that are left unused because they don't match the current societal trends. Accumulation of these items in the home is what results in the development of clutter.

Why the Decluttering Process is Essential

There are numerous reasons why decluttering your home is important. For a quick look at some of these reasons, read on below:

You Create More Space in the Home

Clutter in the home limits the space available in the home. You notice that anytime you try to get around the house, there is always something to impede your movement. These are the effects of having too much clutter around.

Decluttering helps in creating ample space for more valuable objects and activities in the home. Besides the physical impact of clutter in the home, it also affects us mentally. The mental effect of clutter is noticeable in the ease with which you get distracted while working. There are different thoughts that run through your head anytime you see a clutter-filled space while working.

You begin to ponder on things like how to arrange the room, eliminating the clutter, and so on. Decluttering creates space for walking, working, and thinking effectively.

It Becomes Easier to Identify Things of Value

Decluttering is forcing yourself to discard the things you don't need. Once you make up your mind to engage in the decluttering process, you must be selective of things that you keep. There is no room to keep items that you think you will need in the future.

You have to decide whether or not you will read a book that has been lying on your desk for a few months or wear a dress that has been in your wardrobe for the past year. If you decide to discard these items, then it means they were of no value to you from the outset.

You Create a Well-defined Preference

The idea of accumulating various objects and possessions is due to the belief that you need these objects. After making purchases, you find it challenging to make use of these items and keep piling them up in your closet or storage spaces. This includes clothes, shoes, cosmetics, soaps, creams, and so on.

Decluttering will help you find out your preferences. Unlike a cluttered storage space or closet that has numerous designs of clothes, shoes and different brands of cosmetics and soaps, a decluttered home only holds the essential items you need.

This means that the clothes you choose to keep are those that suit your taste, style, and preference. You know more about yourself, such as the materials you love as well as the colors that you fancy.

It Boosts Your Savings

Purchasing and accumulating possessions is one thing, but have you ever considered the cost of owning these items. There are particular objects in the home that need regular maintenance while others cost money to move from one location to another. Decluttering will help you save money on these costs.

It is a Great Way to Earn a Substantial Amount of Money

If you made smart choices during the process of accumulating and purchasing possessions, you have the opportunity to earn a reasonable amount of money when you undertake the decluttering process. Besides donating some of your items, you can choose to sell other items of significant value.

If you are considering putting your house up for sale, it is much easier to execute the sale if the home is decluttered.

It Simplifies the Process of Cleaning

Cleaning is a process that takes a lot of time. The time you spend will double if you have to consider moving clutter from one place to the other before you can clean a particular area. Through the decluttering process, you can rid these areas of clutter for good.

For example, ridding your floating shelf of all the souvenirs and mementos on it means less time spent on dusting.

Freedom to Move Around

The more possessions you own, the more difficult it becomes to relocate. You have to consider how you will pack these items, the cost of transportation, the fragility of the objects, and so on. It also restricts you to a particular size house to ensure there is room for everything you need to move.

Decluttering reduces the amount of stuff you own, and this makes it easy to pack your things and move whenever you want. You will also have an easier time settling into your new home since there are fewer items to unpack and arrange as well as little or no decorations to set up.

The Causes of Home Clutter – And How

We Can Avoid It

Stacks of Paper

One major cause of clutter in the home is the accumulation of excess paper. Paper comes in the form of coupons, mail, magazines, and books. Having any form of paper scattered around the home creates clutter.

How to Avoid and Prevent in the Future

Attending to your letters and mail as soon as they come in can help you avoid the possibility of paper clutter in the home. The first thing you need to do is get a recycling bin and place it close to your front door. This is where you immediately dump junk mail. For those that are of significance, create a filing system to store them neatly.

Old books should be donated or sold to eliminate them from home. You should know that the magazines will keep coming if you still have a subscription. Determine whether there are any magazines that you don't read and ensure you cancel the subscription to these magazines. At this age, you should consider going digital.

Failure to Return Objects to Their Proper Spaces

You can create clutter with things that have value in the home. This is possible if you fail to return these items to their proper position after use.

How to Avoid and Prevent in the Future

Be sure to return each item to its proper position as soon as you are done with it. If your family members are not doing an excellent job with this step, you should encourage them to remove an item or two that don't belong in any room they enter and return it to their appropriate space. Of course, you can try this method as well. Repeat this often, and you can prevent this form of clutter in the future.

Clothes

Severe clutter in the home can also result from how we handle our clothes. The clothes fall into different categories, including used, dirty, and worn clothes. A lot of individuals develop the habit of taking off their clothes and leaving them lying around. You may be one of those individuals that fail to put clothes back into the closet after moderate use.

How to Avoid and Prevent in the Future

The action of leaving clothes lying around after taking them out of the closet may simply be due to lack of space. Create more space by discarding the worn and old clothes in the closet. Also, get over the habit of hanging clothes over the back of a chair when you use them moderately. Creating a rule that you can only take out new clothing after returning the previous clothing helps. As a result, you only have one set of clothing outside the closet at a time. It is also vital you put your dirty clothes in a laundry basket as soon as you take them off.

Thinking That an Item Will Be of Use in the Future

When you think of the possibility of using an item in the future, you tend to keep it around. This makes the item difficult to discard, and having too many of such items creates clutter. It is common for these objects not to be used for anything until they are eventually disposed of.

How to Avoid and Prevent in the Future

Set a deadline for any item you decide to keep for the future. If there is no need for the item in performing any activity around the home by the set deadline, you must discard the item. You have to be realistic. If the deadline is in six months and you don't use it by this time, what is the possibility you will use it in another six months?

Holding on to Items Due to Cost of Purchase

If you spent a lot of money to purchase the item, it is going to be challenging to get rid of it. The majority of people wouldn't feel comfortable in this same situation. However, having a lot of such items around creates clutter in the home.

How to Avoid and Prevent in the Future

Once you have spent money to purchase an item, holding on to it doesn't mean you get your money back. If the item is not useful, then you can't get value out of it. In the future, you must be intentional when making purchases. Any item you are going to spend a large sum of money to get must offer functionalities that you are sure you require.

An Overview of What this Book Will Cover

In this book, you will find out how to adopt a decluttering mindset and the importance of your mindset in achieving success. This mindset change is also essential for progress in various aspects of your life outside of decluttering. Different decluttering activities you will be implementing are explained, including how to properly donate items in your home.

In the chapters that follow, you will learn about some crucial steps that you can take in decluttering each room within the home. Each room has characteristics that there make it unique from the others, and thus require different strategies. We will also tackle how getting rid of items of sentimental value can be difficult and have included a separate chapter to help you get over this challenge.

For those that plan to move to a new home now or in the future, you will find some useful decluttering tips that can help simplify the moving process. If you are not moving anytime soon, you can still make a note to refer to this book when the opportunity to move knocks on your door.

Your Quick Start Action Step:

If your goal is to declutter your home, then it is vital you include it in your schedule. When you have it in your schedule, you start making plans towards completing it. Include your next decluttering session in your Google Calendar to ensure that you get constant reminders. This is a small action that you can take for success in decluttering and other aspects of life.

Chapter 2: The Proper Mindset for Decluttering Success

Chapter 2: The Proper Mindset for Decluttering Success

As individuals, we all have goals or objectives that we plan to achieve sooner or later. Notwithstanding, not everyone will achieve the goals that they have set their sights on. So, what differentiates those that are successful in achieving their goals from those that are not?

The difference in their level of creativity, risk-taking, and intelligence doesn't correctly explain why some people accomplish their goals while others fail. The simple answer is a difference in the mindset of these two separate groups. Those that reach their goals are the individuals that have adopted the right mindset for achieving these goals. The other set of individuals aim for a new goal without making a mindset change.

Now, what is a mindset?

A mindset refers to the various ideas, assumptions, beliefs, and methods that shape the thinking and way of life of an individual. A person's mindset affects how that individual interprets and responds to a situation as well as how they make decisions.

As with a goal you intend to achieve, you need a mindset shift to be successful in decluttering. As a process, it differs significantly from an easy fix to your problems, and you need to understand that it will take a bit of time to reach the results you desire. Due to the time it takes, developing a new set of beliefs is the only way you will be able to see the process through to the end.

Your ability to recognize and accept this fact will be essential in achieving your decluttering goals. There are other things you need to understand about the mindset before we can go over the steps you can take to develop this new mindset that will be beneficial to you.

The research into the relationship between mindset and success by Carol Dweck, a Stanford psychologist, gives a lot of information on the importance of your mindset. A person's mindset can be classified into two main categories, the growth mindset, and the fixed mindset. Knowing the category under which you fall will assist in making the mindset shift you need.

Individuals that have a growth mindset are those that are of the opinion that their basic qualities, abilities, or traits such as intelligence have room for improvements through their hard work. Others with a fixed mindset believe that these qualities or attributes are unalterable, devoid of any possibility of developing further.

The individuals that need a bit of a push are those who have a fixed mindset. It is crucial these individuals learn that there are ways to reshape their thinking. In developing a decluttering mindset, there are specific steps that you can take regardless of your perspective.

These steps are as follows:

1. Accept the Voice of Your Mindset

    Your mindset affects your decision-making process. The decisions you make are usually communicated through a voice in your head. It is through this voice that your mindset becomes evident.

    Do you consider yourself talented enough to achieve this goal? What will others say if you fail? These are some of the things your mindset will communicate through this voice. All these come during times when you are undertaking a new project.

The phrases change when you are unsuccessful in your undertaking. They take a demeaning tone. You could hear your inner voice say, "You wasted so much time decluttering, but your home is still a mess, that's why you need the help of professionals."

If you continually hear negative phrases from the voice, then it means that you have developed a fixed mindset. It undermines your abilities and makes you believe that you should only try to achieve goals that are within your current level.

2. Understand that You Have a Choice

When you give in to the voice, you give up every chance you have to make progress. Know that there is always a choice available to you. Choice represents the way you decide to interpret a situation, criticism, challenges, and setbacks.

You accept that the insufficiencies of your abilities or talents the moment you start interpreting your challenges or setbacks through a fixed mindset. In the interpretation of the growth mindset, your interpretation of a setback is that you should further develop your talents, put in more effort, and adopt a new strategy.

3. Make a Conversation

    The voice of your mindset becomes a loose cannon if you fail to respond appropriately. Your responses should indicate the errors in the assumptions of this voice. Your answer must also reflect that you believe in your abilities.

    Your response should consist of you reassuring yourself, and you can make it as cheeky as you want. Here are some examples of what a fixed mindset says and how to respond using a growth mindset:

- The fixed mindset tells you, "You don't have the talent, don't try it."
- You respond, "My talents may fall short at this moment, but I will put in a lot of effort towards personal development."

Here is another typical example that you have undoubtedly heard at least once in your lifetime:

- "If you fail now, you will remain a failure forever."
- Your response should be, "Failure paves the road to success."

4. Take Action

Thoughts remain just that – thoughts. It is how you decide to implement these thoughts that matters the most. Now, from the previous steps you have taken, you have created a new script that meets your preferences. It is now time to take action following this new script.

The idea is to practice the new thoughts

you have come up with. This is the only way you can determine the effectiveness of your new mindset. Never limit yourself to just reconstructing the negative thoughts in your head. There must be something to show for the changes you have made.

5. Include the Keyword of the Growth Mindset

The growth mindset is all about making positive changes that will take you higher than your current level. It means that a growth phrase is an indication of the progress that you intend to make soon. So, how do you indicate this intention in your phrases?

Simply adding the word, "Yet," to your phrases shows that you have the intention to work towards this goal. It provides the motivation you need to achieve what you say. Using this word, you can easily convert the statements of a fixed mindset to those of a growth mindset.

For example, you can say, "I haven't started decluttering, yet." It means you are training yourself on how to declutter and will be undertaking the process soon.

Benefits of a Mindset change

There are various reasons why you should change your mindset. A number of these reasons relate to your success as an individual. Here are other benefits:

- It promotes persistence and resilience.
- You start to see your limitations not as a hindrance but as opportunities to develop yourself further.
- You have a better handle on any setback.
- You develop a positive attitude towards life.

Your Quick Start Action Step:

The steps to develop a new mindset need to be practiced frequently until they become a part of you. You can schedule a time in the morning or in the evening to perform these steps. Meditating on these steps can also be of significant help.

Chapter 3: Overview of the Decluttering Process

Chapter 3: Overview of the Decluttering Process

In this book, the approach to decluttering has been made as simple as possible to ease the reader into the process. This approach combines the implementation of the small wins strategy in different parts of the home with later advancing to a one-day decluttering session.

The small wins strategy is the main focus of this book since it is the simplest way for anyone to get a proper handle on the decluttering process. In the following chapters, you will learn how to focus on a single room to perform a deep-purge decluttering process.

The one-day cleaning session is a more advanced approach that requires the individual to know a lot about the decluttering process. The skills required are all developed through the small wins strategy, and therefore, it is not an approach to just jump into during the early stages of the decluttering process. In this session, the entire home is decluttered in a single day.

The small wins strategy is one that focuses on smaller parts of the big picture. It is a strategy that becomes vital when looking at the big picture that can hinder your opportunity to make progress. A small win is defined as an objective or goal you achieve that is of minor importance.

Despite being of minor importance, it usually offers motivation to get more work done. As a result, you can perform several small tasks to attain several small wins. By achieving the small victories on a path to a more significant success, the significance of these small wins increases as soon as you complete the main goal.

How to Declutter Your Home When You Are Overwhelmed

Before you start decluttering, and sometimes during the process, you might suddenly become overwhelmed with how much clutter you have to work through. This feeling can make you stop dead in your tracks and makes it difficult to make any progress. In such situations, it is important that you make things as simple as possible.

To start decluttering and overcome the feeling of being overwhelmed, follow these tips to simplify things:

- Choose just 10 minutes of the day to declutter a small area.
- The area you select might be a countertop, shelf, or closet.
- Quickly gather the items creating clutter into a single pile and start picking items from the pile randomly.
- Do I genuinely love this item? Is this something I use frequently? Is it of any use in the home? These are questions that, if answered honestly, will help you identify the real clutter in your home.
- For items that you respond no to, sort them into different labeled boxes. Some items can be given out to someone you know, others recycled, and the rest donated.
- The items you keep are those that you love and those that you use frequently.

- As soon as the timer hits 10 minutes, stop for the day and continue the next day.

The idea of creating just 10 minutes a day to perform decluttering will make it less overwhelming during the early stages. As a result, you look forward to the next day when you can pick up where you left off.

Getting started has been simplified, but it is also important that you create a simple strategy to keep you going. Some tips that you can implement are as follows:

- Continue the process of decluttering in short time bursts.
- The short time frame doesn't give room for perfection, so avoid it. You can always return another time to declutter more.
- Talk to friends to find out which items you can give to them.
- The boxes labeled donate or recycle should be moved to your trunk as soon as they are filled so you remember to get rid of them properly.

- Invite someone you trust to assist since it can be challenging to make sound judgment when it comes to getting rid of your possessions.
- Items that you think you may need should go into a box labeled "maybe". On this box, also include the date you put the items into the box. Any item that remains in the box for at least six months should be discarded.

The free space you create after decluttering can also serve as motivation to keep moving forward. Take some time to take in the view, enjoy it, and get attached to this sort of simplicity in your home.

Donating Items You No Longer Need

When you decide to declutter, it is challenging to accept that you will be throwing items in the trash. It is more challenging when the items in question are those that you feel are valuable despite being useless in your home. To change your views to a more positive perspective, it is crucial you consider donating some of the items that you don't think should be thrown out.

There are different ways to donate items, including giving to people around you who are sure to value these items. Regardless, not everything will find a home among your immediate circle of friends or family members.

When you decide to donate, knowing some of the places that accept these donations can be very helpful. There are also specific tips on how to make the donation more appealing to those that need it. This section focuses on certain items that you can donate regularly.

Clothes

A lot of people spend large amounts of money to acquire clothes, so it is understandable when they find it difficult to let go of them even though they are not in use. Giving your unused clothing up for the right cause should offer the motivation you need.

You can keep a special box or donation bag to stuff with clothes you no longer use. Once the bag is full, look for a charity you love and make a donation.

You can visit any of these places to donate your clothes:

- Salvation Army International
- Goodwill Clothing & Donation Centers
- Vietnam Veterans of America

A simple step you can take is to clean the clothes before making a donation. Remember that someone, somewhere, will be smiling thanks to your act of goodwill.

Books

The books you must donate are those that you are sure you are not going to read. It is essential you give them out so they can make their way to homes where they will be of actual value. You should check between the pages of these books to make sure you didn't leave any paper or notes behind before donating them.

Some places you can donate books include:

- The local library
- Operation Paperback

- Access Books
- Schools in your community

Books are easy to pack for donations; one good way is to place unused books in a box. To ensure you make the donation, don't move this box back into a storage area but take it directly to your car as soon as it is full.

Old Cell Phones

The common step people take in getting rid of cell phones is to put it in a drawer or box and store it away. These phones are usually forgotten and only make an appearance during the decluttering process.

To provide value to others in need, check out these donation centers:

- American Cell Phone Drive
- ReCellular
- Cell Phone for Soldiers

Remember to clear your personal data before giving out your old cell phones.

Tools

You are likely going to have lots of tools that are

due for donations. We commonly purchase tools for a specific project that then become useless once the project is complete. Rather than letting them gather dust and take up space in your home, you can donate these tools.

Packing your tools for donations is quite straightforward since most of these tools usually come in boxes. Find a box to pack those without one.

Construction-focused charities like Habitat for Humanity will be willing to accept these donations.

Computers

Just because a computer is old doesn't mean it is not in good enough condition for use. If you want to make an impact, your old computers can be put to good use in local libraries and schools within your community.

Unless you engage in a computer exchange program to get new computers, you can donate your old computers to these schools and libraries. It is essential you wipe the computer hard drive before making a donation. You can't count on someone else to do the right thing when they find the information you leave behind.

Furniture

The furniture in your home includes some of the items that are always useful to someone else. Recycling furniture is something that happens only on rare occasions, so there is always a need for donated furniture. Check the furniture for nails sticking out, clean, and dust it before making your donation.

Places that accept furniture donations include the following:

- Operation Homefront
- Furniture Banks
- Salvation Army

Linens

Linens are items that you can choose to donate along with the various clothing items in your home. If you are an animal lover and decide to donate your linens separately, you can make your animal friends happy by donating to an animal shelter. They are essential for use in bathing animals and making bed linings.

Make a call to the local shelter to ensure they are accepting linens before making the trip. Also, wash the items before donating them.

Kitchen Appliances

Kitchen appliances usually occupy a lot of space in the kitchen. This can become a clutter problem when they are not in use. It is an excellent idea to give away the appliances that you no longer use.

If you decide to donate rather than recycle these appliances, you should make sure you get the cord and other attachments that go along with the appliance to make it useful to whoever receives it.

Cars

If you know the money doesn't matter to you, then you can choose to donate your old cars rather than have them recycled or sell them. In addition to the good you are doing; a tax write-off is a benefit you enjoy from this action.

You can look to these areas to make a car donation:

- Car Talk Vehicle Donation Program
- Car Donation Center

It is necessary to get the car properly cleaned before making the donation. This also gives you the opportunity to find documents and receipts that contain information you don't want to expose.

Your Quick Start Action Step:

Take your first step towards decluttering by engaging yourself in the decluttering of a small space using the small wins strategy. You should also try to implement the various tips given for donating some of your items.

"Declutter Your Life: Simple Decluttering Strategies on How to Declutter and Organize your Life to Free Yourself from Worry and Enjoy Stress-Free Living" is another book by me that gives you more information on how to build a lifestyle focused on decluttering. For those who have a desire to create this sort of lifestyle, you can find the book on the online store.

Chapter 4: Living Room and Family Room

Chapter 4: Living Room and Family Room

Depending on the size of the home, it is common to have either both a living room and family room or just a living room. Larger houses with enough space to spare usually make this distinction while other, smaller homes opt to make efficient use of space by combining the living room with the family room.

In homes where these rooms are separate, the living room has a more formal design while the family room is informal. The formal model of the living room makes it an excellent place for receiving any guests that visit. Regarding its location, it is typical for the living room to be the first room that anyone who enters the house steps into. As a result, there is no need for visitors to get too far into the house to hold a conversation.

The family room is a more informal set-up that is frequently accessed by family members. In this room, you find various items like the television and game consoles that make it the right location for entertainment and other activities like studying and reading. In addition to the comfortable design that promotes social interactions and relaxation, it is also the right place for kids to play around. Since most home designs place the family room close to the kitchen, parents can monitor the kids while they work.

Since all the family members make use of these rooms, it is a challenge to keep them clutter-free at all times. Regardless, you first need to eliminate the most significant sources of clutter in these areas to make progress. Clutter will make it very difficult for these spaces to offers a spot for relaxation to any member of the family.

Steps to Take

1. Purge Items That Shouldn't Be in the Space

   There are various things that we keep in these rooms that are out of place. Your paperwork, exercise equipment, unused toys, ornaments, and decorations. These are just a few of the items creating clutter in these rooms.

The first step in decluttering is to purge these items. This step is simple to implement and reduces your workload as you progress with the decluttering process. As a space for relaxation, it is common for members of the family to enter these rooms with items that they can use in relaxing. However, the family member should take these items back to their proper location when they leave.

2. Create Additional Storage

While there are lots of items that you shouldn't keep in these areas, some items must remain here. For such items, having designated storage is essential in reducing the clutter they create. Examples of these items include toys, books, blankets, remotes, and video games.

Vertical storage is an option that you mustn't overlook. You can start by installing shelves that will be useful in storing your entertainment devices like

DVDs and video games. A bookshelf is also an excellent addition that can store your books, magazines, and office supplies in a neat and organized manner depending on how effectively you utilize it.

For the toys, you may look to save money since there is probably a toy box in each child's bedroom. In actuality, having a smaller toy box in the living room will save you from the noise and pain that you experience when stepping on different toys. The toys you keep in this box are those that the kids frequently use anytime you need them around for close supervision.

Creating a clutter-free space is about making the most of anything you own. You can do this by investing in storage ottomans. These function as footstools or stools while still offering internal storage. They are useful in keeping things like magazines and remotes out of sight.

Remote controls and toys often get broken. It is vital you discard these broken items quickly.

3. Go Minimalist With Your Decoration

An excellent way to create clutter in the living room is through your decorating strategy. Decorations that creates clutter include hanging pictures, shadow box art, and excess couch pillows. The stacked books trend is also a decorating style that builds clutter.

A simple action you could take is removing a number of pillows. You should also install floating shelves. These are useful in arranging your pictures and other mementos. You can, of course, donate or re-home decorations that you believe fail to add enjoyment to the space.

4. Decide How You Will Eliminate Items of Value

Some items that create clutter are still of value. In this case, you need to implement a strategy to either donate or sell these items. If you have a collection of DVDs, books, or CDs, you can give them to someone who needs them or sells them to those willing to pay for them.

The contents of DVDs and CDs vary from movies and videos to music and audiobooks. To ensure you don't have any need to retain these items, convert the contents to a digital format. The benefit of this action is to minimize the need for more shelves.

5. Clear Wire Clutter

An entertainment center is an integral part of these home spaces. The problem with the setup is the level of clutter the wires produce. Cord management is an important activity that will help rid the home of this problem. There are numerous steps you can take towards decluttering your cables.

Feeding wires through the wall is one of the simplest methods to rid the cable clutter in the home. Nonetheless, it may not appeal to you as an individual. Although not the best option, you can use the option of covering wires with furniture to clear the visual clutter.

Clearing out cords is not a realistic option so you must come up with creative ways to keep them out of sight. Some excellent choices include the use of area rugs around areas where the cord clutter is focused. Another option is to get a box, container, or basket that you can put the excess lengths of cord in. Matching this container or box to the living room décor will make it more visually appealing.

The last option you have is limit the length of cables and cords you use in setting up your entertainment systems. If the wires are too long, it increases the difficulty you will have in managing the clutter they create.

6. Furniture

This is vital in beautifying your

living/family room and making it comfortable for anyone that intends to relax. Besides the beauty, you must also consider the size of the furniture you fit into these rooms. These are usually the items that create the most clutter in the home.

During the selection of furniture, you should pick sizes that don't make the rooms feel overloaded. You should also consider the use of floating shelves to improve airflow and reduce ground clutter. Remember, don't install excess.

Your Quick Start Action Step:

The living room or family room has a lot of open space that you can declutter with ease. Simply go into the room with a box and a trash basket for a quick declutter. The box will be used in packing items that don't belong in the room while the trash basket is for items that need to leave the home. You can do this in 20 minutes and organize the room within 10 minutes.

Chapter 5:
Bedrooms

Chapter 5: Bedrooms

The bedroom is a home space for relaxation and recovery of energy after a stressful day of work. To ensure you enjoy your period of relaxation and recovery, it is essential that the bedroom is free of clutter. Despite the need for a clutter-free bedroom, there are various reasons why clutter piles up in this room.

The decluttering strategy that will be of great benefit when working on the bedroom is the four-box method. In this method, you need to get your hands on four boxes that will each serve a unique purpose as you work through the clutter in the bedroom. The labels on each box are as follows:

- Put Away: These are items that are out of place in the bedroom. Any item that has its appropriate storage like a cup that should be in the kitchen and documents from the home office all go into this box.
- Donate/Sell: The items that make their way into this box are those that are no longer of use in your home. Although you

don't need them, these items still retain their value. To make the most of the value they offer, you can decide to either sell or donate these items. Selling gets you a little cash while donating helps those in need.

- Storage: Some of the things creating clutter in your room are things that you don't use often. Pile up this box and move it to your storage room once it is fully packed.
- Trash: In reality, this box is a trash can. Items that are damaged beyond repair and without value are thrown into the trash for proper disposal.

Engaging in The Process

The steps you should take when decluttering the bedroom are given below:

1. Take Out Items and Group Them Into the Boxes

    As mentioned earlier, you are using the four-box method to enable the effective decluttering of your bedroom. You need to take out everything that is in your bedroom to have a proper look as you sort through these items. The easiest items to identify are those that are going into the trash. Items like broken ornaments, damaged clothes, and old shoes should be discarded.

Separate items that you need to take to your storage space. These items are also quite easy to identify. For a simple tip, any item that you haven't used in the last six months should go into the storage box. These are additional items creating unnecessary clutter in the bedroom.

You are sure to find items in your room that are suitable for donating and those that will fetch a reasonable price if you decide to sell them. These items go into the donate/sell box. Here you put things like books and clothes that you know are still useful, but you won't be needing for a long time. This action helps you make the most of your possessions rather than letting them get damaged.

2. Clear the Clutter on the Nightstand and Other Flat Surfaces

The clutter that builds up on your nightstand and other flat surfaces in the home can consist of decorations, books, pens, tissue boxes, and so on. Get to work on these items immediately to get rid of a massive amount of clutter.

The box with the 'Put Away' label is useful at this stage of the decluttering process. Mail and paperwork from your office should go here along with books that you have completed. These items have their appropriate storage spaces within the home so you can take them back after decluttering the bedroom.

Taking out items for recycling is another excellent step to rid the room of clutter. These items include your dried-out pens, old chargers, and tissue boxes. Small objects like this can pile up if you don't take swift action to eliminate them.

The items discussed above are frequently observed on your nightstand. So once you've tackled them, it is time for other flat surfaces in the bedroom. Certain surfaces may be impossible to completely rid of clutter. In such instances, make sure you arrange objects in moderation.

There should be a limit to the pictures, decorations, and lamps you have in the bedroom. A single lamp on your nightstand or dresser can function effectively when you need to read a book. A good action plan is to ensure that each surface in the bedroom doesn't contain more than five items.

3. Tackle the Drawers in the Room

A vanity table or bureau in your bedroom will usually contain drawers that hide a lot of clutter. Take your time in going through these drawers. You mustn't rush the decluttering process.

If you are taking time to declutter, you can avoid the urge to hide more clutter inside these drawers. The simple phrase, out of sight, out of mind, applies to this situation.

As you work your way through each of the drawers, remove the items in each drawer and sort through them. Items that are going back into the drawers should be folded and well organized. Those that are leaving should be put in the donate/sell box. Others go straight into the trash. Questions you can ask yourself to simplify the separation process are as follows:

- Did I make use of it in the last six months?
- Should it be in my bedroom?
- Will it be of value if I donate it?

The answers you give for each question will determine whether you want to donate, discard, sell, or put away the item. After separating items into boxes, you have to return whatever is left into the drawers. Small containers and dividers can help organize the drawer into compartments — these help in keeping similar items in the same partition.

4. Seasonal Items

Decorations, beddings, and clothing that are only useful in a particular season should be kept out of sight to avoid creating clutter. These objects will not be used for months, so is there a need to have these items lying around in the bedroom?

Excellent decluttering actions you can take for such items is to find a cloth bin, comforter bag, plastic, or space-saver bag to fit in these articles. Once you have them in a proper form of storage, find a space to keep them. Under your bed is a great place to store these items since you won't be needing them for a while.

5. Take Out Furniture You Don't Need

Your bedroom is for one sole purpose, and that is for recovery from the day's work. What this means is that the furniture you have in this space should only be the essentials you require to rest and prepare for the day. It is time to identify the furniture that meets these requirements and take out the rest.

If you want to enjoy a period when you can relax and recharge, then having a work desk in your bedroom won't do you much good. When you turn over, and you see a desk stacked with paperwork reminding you of unpaid bills and uncompleted projects, your chances of getting a good night's rest decline.

The size of the furniture is also an important aspect to consider. The smaller the furniture, the more space is offered and the less-cluttered the bedroom appears. It gives you additional floor space for movement.

6. Kids Toys

If you are thinking of piling up the kid's toys in a closet, then you are robbing yourself of valuable storage space in the home. The toys can fit into a bin, basket, or toy chest – a product that was designed solely for this purpose.

As you keep purchasing new toys and piling them up in the home, you notice that, in addition to clutter, you are quickly running out of storage space. A toy chest cannot serve as a great decluttering tool if you end up stacking multiple chests in the room. The toy chest running out of space is a clear sign that it is time to dispose of some toys.

Kids can be very observant when it comes to their toys, but that doesn't mean you can't cleverly discard some of these toys. You can start by removing a few toys and see how they react over the next week. If there is no reaction, then you can donate or discard these toys. Repeat the process until you have a manageable number of toys left. Or get the child involved in the decluttering process themselves.

7. Clean Out Your Closet

The closet is an essential architectural addition in the bedroom. It is crucial to the proper organization and arrangement of clothes and shoes in the home. It can also be one of the places where you keep a lot of clutter in the bedroom.

The clutter that develops in the closet is often due to the excess clothes and shoes you possess. Besides the clutter issue this excess causes, you also have to deal with the problem of selecting clothes to wear daily. You should reduce the number of articles of clothing in your closet to make things easier.

Simple steps you can take include donating clothes and shoes that don't fit or throwing them in the trash depending on the state of the items. The organization of the closet is also a crucial part of the decluttering process. More on this will be discussed in a later chapter.

Your Quick Start Action Step:

First, create a schedule and plan out the day it is

most convenient to declutter.

If you want to declutter the kids' room quickly, simply get rid of the toys on the floor that make it difficult to walk with ease. This is often the real cause of clutter in your children's bedroom.

For the adult's bedroom, clear the top of the dressers and nightstands while packing the dirty clothes in a basket and other items that don't belong here in a box. Remember to make the bed during the process to give the bedroom a great appearance.

Chapter 6: Kitchen

Chapter 6: Kitchen

Most of the activities in the home take place in the kitchen. Depending on the layout of the house, the kitchen will be one of the areas that you can easily access from the living room or family room. Since it is where you install your refrigerator, you can expect a lot of traffic into the kitchen.

This high traffic makes the kitchen a magnet for clutter in the home. Clutter often appears in the form of personal belongings left behind by family members, dishes, paperwork, and mail. It is also quite common to find several appliances on the kitchen countertops. Besides, this is where you drop your grocery bags and start distributing items after going shopping.

Due to the various functions it offers as well as the numerous storage spaces in the form of cupboards, refrigerator, and pantry, it is essential that you declutter your kitchen regularly. Surface decluttering is usually quite straightforward since you are going for items on the counter, but you need to go a bit further when you decide to do a deep purge declutter.

Considering the size of the kitchen, the best strategy you can apply is the divide and conquer decluttering strategy. This strategy allows you to focus on one storage area of the kitchen before moving to the next. In the topics that follow, we will take a look at how to declutter the kitchen pantry, refrigerator, cupboards, countertops, tools, and under the sink. So, let us get started.

1. Decluttering Your Pantry

    The pantry is a cupboard in which you store provisions, food, cleaning chemicals, or beverages in the kitchen. In some homes, the pantry is the same as a cupboard while it is separate in others. It is easy to gather excess items in the pantry when you purchase new stock of something without checking what you have left.

    Here are some simple steps you can take to declutter the pantry:

- The first step is to eliminate excesses from the pantry. An easy way to determine what items you need dispose of is to identify those that are beyond their expiry date. You should also check through the items inside the pantry to find and throw out those that have been infested by pests.
- If you want to use the pantry solely for food and beverages, then you need to take out any other items like cutlery sets, cups, and so on.
- Separate the items such as spices, ingredients, and food that you are sure you won't use. Some baking spices are common culprits in this case.
- Foodstuffs that are not expired but will not be used in the home should be donated. Visit a food bank to give out these items so they can serve those in need.

- Learn to combine similar items into the same package or use mason jars. Mason jars are excellent for storing spices and cereals to reduce the number of containers you have to organize in the pantry.

2. Decluttering Tips For the Fridge

The fridge is an integral part of your kitchen. It is where you store leftovers and fresh food to prevent them from going bad. It is quite common to forget certain items you store in the fridge if you don't need them for a long time. These items are a part of the reason why you must declutter your fridge.

For steps to take in decluttering your fridge, read on below:

- Remove all the items in the fridge to start the decluttering process.
- Once emptied, ensure you clean the fridge properly.

- Look for food items that have gone bad, including vegetables, fruits, and leftovers in the fridge since it is possible that these items made their way to the back as you added more things into the fridge, making them difficult to see.
- Empty the fridge by throwing out food items that you don't enjoy using along with spreads, condiments, and dressings that are expired.
- You should also extend this process to food items or ingredients that you only need for a once in a year recipe. These are likely to expire before the next use so make sure you toss them out.
- If you have an excess number of the same foodstuff such as baked beans or ketchup, you can give some out to others to reduce the level of clutter in the fridge.

- Implement the use of plastic or glass containers in storing leftover food in the fridge. These containers offer a see-through feature that makes it easy to identify the item inside and are also durable.

3. Decluttering Your Kitchen Tools

    Handheld tools that serve various cooking and food preparation functions are referred to as cooking tools. It is easy to have an excess number of these items since they are small and very affordable.

    Other small electrical appliances and gadgets such as handheld electric mixers, timers, and thermometers also fall within this category. There are specific steps that you can follow to declutter these tools effectively:

    - First, remove items that don't belong in the storage space of your utensils. Depending on your kitchen arrangement, these may be cups, plates, or gadgets from another room.

- Get rid of tools that are missing a part and those that are broken.
- Using your cooking habits as a guide, identify the gadgets and utensils as well as the frequency with which you use these items in a day. This approach helps determine the essential number of these tools that need to be available for use before the next wash.
- Gadgets and utensils that you don't use regularly should be donated. Don't try keeping that juice extractor for another six months in the hopes you'll finally use it.
- Reduce the number of serving utensils in the home if you don't get visitors often. Four soup ladles may not be necessary and will end up creating clutter.

4. Decluttering Under the Kitchen Sink

The space under the sink is where most people store their cleaning supplies. It often accumulates clutter because, despite buying more items, some products under the sink rarely get used. Since it is usually out of sight, it is more challenging to keep track of what you have.

To clear the clutter under your kitchen sink, you can follow these steps:

- Clear out and avoid buying single-use products like descalers and specialist drain cleaners.
- Replace the use of window cleaners, oven top cleaners, cream cleaners, etc. with the use of microfiber cloths.
- Get rid of highly toxic cleaners that are harmful to pets and kids.
- Shift to the use of reusable cloths and get rid of the pile of disposable scrubbers and cloths under the sink.

- Specialist laundry products should be eliminated from the home. Instead, opt for gentle laundry liquids.
- Discard any item that you haven't made use of in the last 12 months.

5. Decluttering the Cupboards

Since the kitchen usually contains a large number of items, it is common to have all your various cupboards full of different things, including foodstuffs, canned products, dishes, appliances, and so on. It also means you need to declutter the cabinets from time to time. Some easy steps you can take are as follows:

- Pull out all the items in a cupboard.
- Take stock of all the things you pull out and then inspect each item.
- During the inspection, identify items that are expired so they can immediately be thrown away.

- Separate the items that you don't need any longer and those that have been sitting in the cupboard for months. The useable items should be given away.
- Use this opportunity to clean the cabinets with a damp cloth.
- Rearrange the remaining items in the cupboards neatly. For small pieces, you can implement the use of wire baskets.
- You can buy matching canisters that you can stack neatly for storing items.
- Consider shifting to the open shelving method so you can see what you have at a glance.

6. Decluttering Your Kitchen Countertops

The countertops in the kitchen are the most accessible place to drop your shopping bags and other items once you step into the kitchen. This approach makes them an attractive area for clutter. Clearing clutter on the countertops can be quite easy since the entire space is visible.

Here are some easy steps you can take to complete this process:

- Move the items creating clutter to the floor or your dining table.
- Get a cleaning cloth and soapy water to clean the countertop.
- Inspect the things you have moved from the countertops and separate those that you can donate as well as those that are better off in a different room.
- Move some of the items into various cupboards in the kitchen.
- If your storage space is limited, create zones on the countertop with each zone assigned a selection of similar items.
- Frequently used appliances like a coffee maker or blender can find a spot on the countertop.
- Avoid piling dishes and mail on the countertops.

Your Quick Start Action Step:

Doing the dishes as soon as you are done with your meal or at the end of the day can prevent the pile-up of clutter. Reducing the number of silverware in the kitchen also goes a long way in minimizing clutter. You can quickly get rid of the appliances taking a spot on the countertops if they are not in use.

All these tasks should be included in your daily schedule.

Chapter 7: Bathrooms and Laundry Room

Chapter 7: Bathrooms and Laundry Room

Bathroom

When it comes to bathrooms, decluttering involves removing and organizing the items which take up space in your drawers, shelves, and countertops. It can be surprising to finally find out just how many things you have and how many you have to wade through to find the ones that you need.

Follow these guidelines when deciding to declutter your bathroom:

1. Empty Your Bathroom Drawers and Closet of Everything In Them

   When it comes to decluttering, specific experts have recommended going through this process with as many bathrooms as you have at once. This method helps you gain a clear idea of just how much extra stuff you have. For instance, you might have enough bathroom soap to last the year and not be aware of it. Whichever way you aim to do this, it is vital to clear the countertops, clean out the drawers, and thoroughly clean the linen closets in and around your bathrooms.

2. Get Rid of Duplicates

   Getting rid of duplicates such as extra brushes, thermometers, hair dyes, body scrubbers, loofahs, and more is a great way to declutter your bathroom. You should get rid of the old items once you purchase new items to replace them. This strategy helps you avoid the build-up of clutter. You should always be aware of things such as extra conditioner, shampoo, body lotion, bar soap, and other skincare products. Make a list of anything that has not been used in six months and get rid of them.

3. Place Similar Items Together

   Doing this is a vital step when it comes to organizing and decluttering your bathroom. Make a pile for towels, medicine, cleaning supplies, toiletries, makeup, etc. this helps you to see what you are aiming to remove from your bathroom.

4. Reduce your Counter Clutter

   Once you have decided which things you make use of and want to keep, you should put the items that you make use of daily in easy to access locations. Your counters should remain clear and should only contain toothbrushes, hand soap, and toothpaste. If there is not enough storage space, you can make use of a storage box to hold a couple of items. That being said, you should not attempt to turn your counter into a storage space.

5. Cleaning Supplies

   You should ensure that everything you keep is something that you find useful. Sponges and brushes that are too old to use should be thrown away. It takes a bit of time to finish a container of cleaner, which is why it is imperative to ensure that you do not have too many surplus items.

Organize your bathroom and ensure it stays that way.

Essential tools for organizing your bathroom are drawer organizers, dividers, small baskets, and boxes. With numerous small items located in the bathroom, it would be time-wasting, not to mention frustrating, if you have to go through every drawer to find the one thing you need. Organizing the clutter in your bathroom is not something that costs money. Search for small containers or plastics located all over the house which can be repurposed into drawer organizers. As with other spaces in the home, you aim to eradicate as many items as possible from your bathroom's countertops. If the items are used daily, they should be neatly organized in a container or placed in a drawer that can be easily accessed.

6. Get Rid of or Donate Any Excess

Most times when decluttering, we discover that there are various containers or bottles of half-empty things in our bathrooms. When we have more than one of the same item, it is best to put them together and get rid of the empty containers or bottles. If you find yourself holding onto an item that has a little bit left, you should give yourself a time limit of a month to use the item. If it not used within that month, it has to be thrown away.

Another item that could be creating bathroom clutter is towels. Most times, we purchase new towels to replace the supposedly worn-out ones. However, we never get rid of the old ones leading us to accumulate more and more of them. Decide what a perfectly suitable number of towels would be for your home. Maybe you can make use of 8 bath towels. It is an excellent number for a family of 3 with two extra towels able to serve any guests or act as spares.

7. Cosmetics

Cosmetics should never be kept for an indefinite period as they are capable of growing bacteria or even expiring. Using them at that point could have adverse consequences. The majority of cosmetics should only be kept for a maximum of a year.

8. Hair Products

   There have been periods when I stumbled upon 5-year-old hair gel. One way that we build up clutter in our bathroom is by purchasing a new product to see if it will work for you. After using it, you notice that it doesn't. However, since it would feel incredibly wasteful to throw them away, you keep them only to stumble upon it five years later. You have to get rid of it, especially if you can't remember when you purchased it or when the last time was that someone used it.

9. Prescriptions

   It is imperative to throw away any old medicines not being used by anyone. These old prescriptions do nothing but create clutter, and they can also be dangerous if used. Certain pharmacies allow people to turn in old prescriptions.

10. Over the Counter Medication

    Things like pain killers, ointments, and creams all come with an expiration date printed on them. These items don't last as long as we think they do. When decluttering, it is not uncommon to come across medication or creams that have expired many years ago. If it is a medication you need to have on standby, you can add it to the shopping list and ensure you replace it.

11. Stock Ups

    It is usual for a bathroom to have a stash of items that were purchased due to being on sale. These stock ups have to be decluttered. You have to ensure anything you decide to stock up on is a product that your family uses. You also have to make sure that it will be placed somewhere that makes it visible and available for use before it sits in storage and expires.

12. Skincare Products

    These products have to be used every day or at the very least weekly, and if you are not using it as frequently, then you have no need for it. Everyone has face washes, creams, and lotions that were purchased for the sole purpose of making us look youthful, only for them to be relegated to the back of the drawer when we realized it was all a marketing gimmick. You should only store the things that you are using.

13. Hair Accessories

    When decluttering your bathroom, you should go through any pins, hair ties, headbands, scarfs, and other hair accessories to ensure that they are still usable. If you discover anything that is broken, you should throw it out. You should fight the urge to put overstretched hair ties back in your drawers. They should be thrown out once they outlive their usefulness to prevent clutter.

14. Appliances

You might have a non-working electric shaver stored in the bathroom for no reason other than to collect dust. Decluttering gives you the time to realize when you are unable to make good use of a particular appliance, and it would be better if you got rid of it, sold it, or donated it.

15. Travel Samples and Size

    You might believe that it is particularly wasteful to get rid of travel-sized items and samples, right? Most times, we keep them somewhere making a mental note to use them on our next trip, but we end up forgetting about them. It is not surprising to find samples older than some of your clothes in a bathroom. The old stuff should be thrown out. If possible, you should donate the unopened items or make use of them. Another way to cut down on waste is not to purchase a new item and make use of the travel-sized item until it is finished.

16. Counter Clutter

You should have a look and make a list of the things that seem to reside on your counter permanently. Ascertain that they deserve to be in that place. We often make a conscientious effort to keep nothing but face wash and hand soap on their bathroom counters because when you decide to add one more thing, it doesn't just end at one more thing. When you have a clear bathroom counter, everyone in that household can understand that there should not be anything left out. It should be put away once it is done being used.

17. Kid Stuff

    Bath toys and other age-appropriate stuff should only be kept in the bathroom if the child that owns those things needs them when taking a bath.

Laundry Room

Let's be honest with ourselves for a second: almost every one of us hates having to do laundry. It could be because of how much time it requires, how much it interrupts the day, or just because it is an incredibly mundane task. Trust me. You are not alone. There are quite a lot of people that feel just like this. For most homeowners, the bone of contention isn't quite the act itself; instead, it is because their laundry room is cramped, small, or just plain uninviting. It might appear as an afterthought, but learning how you can organize the place where you do your laundry is a critical step in ensuring the house stays clean. In the majority of homes, a laundry room doubles as a tight space for clothes, piles, towels, and shoes. All that will change because this article is going to show you how you can completely re-vamp your laundry room into one that is organized, welcoming, and functional.

1. Develop Laundry Stations

   Do you have a dedicated space where you store your hampers? Is there a dedicated space to not only fold but sort out laundry? Do you often find yourself carrying a big pile of clothes up and down the stairs with nowhere to place them?

This space is where organized laundry spaces or stations earn their keep. Nevertheless, before you can organize, you have to create a system that enables you and everyone else in the household to maintain that room's clutter-free, clean, and spacious state.

You should use the following variables as guidelines when creating a functional laundry station:

2. Counter Space

   The whole point of organizing is to make your life simpler. One way of doing that is to have sufficient access to folding tables or counter space. When you have available counter space, you are more inclined to fold, hang, and put your clothes away once they are taken out of the dryer or washer.

3. Drying Rack

   It does not matter if you prefer to dry your clothes on a drying rack or hangers; you must make at least one of these spaces available. You can also make use of tension rods to dry your clothes if you are space conscious.

4. Laundry Baskets

   Ensure you have a laundry basket or hamper situated in your laundry room. This approach helps you to unload and load your items quickly while doing laundry. Generally, these can be placed either in a closet nearby or underneath your counters.

5. Ironing Board

   Rather than storing wrinkled clothes away and then ironing them right before you have to wear them, you should have an ironing board situated in the laundry room. This action helps you unwrinkle your outfits faster. Doing this not only saves you time and hassle but also saves space in the long-term.

6. Make the Most of the Space You Already Have

   A laundry room is supposed to be solely for washing, drying, and ironing our clothes, however, it ends up serving as a multipurpose room. It stores our coats, towels, shoes, pet supplies, backpacks, and more. A great way to organize all of these items is to make use of vertical storage. Vertical storage enables you to make the most of your available space while keeping it uncluttered.

Make use of every bit of space the laundry room has by using shelves, wall units, and hanging baskets. See below for more details on how to maximize the use of your laundry room:

Make use of wall space

Certain people see the laundry room as an entry point into the house, which is why it is imperative to have dedicated areas for your shoes, irrespective of the season. DIY shoe racks can be a way to stop anyone from tracking in dirt and grass through the house. These racks are easy to set up and also cost-effective. They can be manufactured from floating shelves, tension rods, or PVC pipes. They can also be stored on a solid wall.

You can invest in hooks, baskets, and

shelves

They are simple solutions that make it seamless for you to store your items while also preventing the build-up of clutter. Dryer sheets and laundry detergents can be placed in wire racks or shelving above the dryer and washer. Jackets, backpacks, hats, and accessories can be stored on hooks placed on the wall.

Smaller things can be placed inside decorative baskets. This step ensures the floor space remains open and clean.

A great way to maximize your space is to consider any hidden storage that might not be so apparent. You might consider hanging items over the door. The laundry room door is not just for keeping the noise down. Its back can become a beautiful place to store an ironing board until it is required. This way of storing items is even made more straightforward thanks to over the door storage organizers which enable you to keep your things out of view.

Select the correct laundry storage solution

Learning the proper way to organize a laundry room is not just about cleaning and then moving things around. Once you figure out how you can make the most out of your space and also create the required number of laundry stations, you have to make sure that you have the storage containers capable of handling your laundry supplies.

Consider purchasing the following containers to have the best solution for your laundry room storage:

Closed containers are useful to help hide away your laundry essentials. They also ensure the room looks much more organized. Open containers can be used to store bleach bottles and laundry detergent boxes.

Canvas containers or lined baskets can be used to clean up after spills.

Small items such as stain sticks, pocket change, lone socks, and laundry markers can be stored using small boxes. You should ensure that these containers can easily be accessed when you are in your laundry room. This effort not only helps to keep your dedicated spaces organized, but it also hides the laundry essentials from guests when they come over.

Consider purchasing appliances that help to save space

It is true, dryers and washers tend to take up a lot of space; however, that does not mean we should give up and let them take over the laundry room. This tip is a great idea to go with if you are in the market for a new dryer or washer. It is also great if you are looking to downsize to a smaller yet more efficient appliance. You should always remember that less can be more. Using a smaller dryer or washer could give you more space to work within your laundry room and your home at large. It could also create an area that is much more functional for your household.

There are numerous benefits to purchasing a washer and dryer combo appliance:

- You can fit your smaller stacked devices into smaller spaces such as closets, apartments, or studios.

- Smaller dryers and washers tend to be equipped with bottom drawers which provide additional hidden storage.
- Dryers and washers that save space do more than just that. They are particularly efficient, which helps to save on the utility bills as well as reduce your carbon footprint, and save the environment.

Your Quick Start Action Step:

Clearing out expired medications in the bathroom and empty containers of soap and other items can free up a lot of space.

A laundry basket in the laundry room is also a tremendous help to properly store your laundry. You can use this in limiting clutter on the floors.

Chapter 8: Closets

Chapter 8: Closets

The closet is a vital storage space in the home in which you can keep your clothes, shoes, and other items out of sight. Since the items inside are not visible, it is easy to overlook the clutter you create inside the closet.

When decluttering, you should try to simplify the process by decluttering based on the type of clothing you have in the closet. To this end, you need to categorize the objects into boots, denim, dresses, shoes, coats, and so on. You should understand that it is much simpler to identify the dresses that you don't need anymore when you are looking at all the dresses you own rather than a mix of your dresses and jeans collection.

How to Declutter Your closets

1. Take Out the Items in the Closet

    This is a step that simplifies your decluttering process. As soon as you take out the objects filling up the closet, you can identify those that are in the wrong storage space. Out of the pile of clothes and other objects from the cabinet, these identified items should be screened out.

Clearing out the closet provides the opportunity to clean the interior of the cabinets properly.

2. Discard Some Items

    Regardless of the number of clothes or shoes you own, there will only be a few of these that you wear most of the time. This tip gives you room to rid your closets of most of the clothes and shoes that you store in them. If you are finding it difficult to reach a decision, answering these questions can help:

    - Did you wear it on any day during the last six months?
    - Is the item faded, stained, or torn?
    - Is it still an excellent fit?

    Clothing articles you need to get rid of are easily identifiable through the answers you give to these questions.

3. Move Your Seasonal Clothes

   Seasonal clothes take up a reasonable amount of space in the closet but don't get used often. You can move seasonal clothes and shoes into a storage box or bin to create space in the closet. The bin can be kept under the bed or in a storage room until the contents are required.

4. Organize the Closet from the Bottom and Move Towards the Top

   When rearranging the objects back into the closet, you should start arranging from the bottom of the closet and work your way to the objects that will be at the top. The simple reason for this is to prevent interference from hanging clothes as you try to put the closet in order.

5. Learn to Make Use of Vertical Spaces

   Adding a new closet for more storage is usually not an option. Instead, you can make the most of what's already in place. The back of the closet door, top of the shelf, and wall offer excellent storage opportunities if adequately utilized. You can hang your scarves, robes, jewelry, and other items on hooks. Besides, rather than an entire closet, you can add a shelf at the top for objects that you need on special occasions.

6. Incorporate the Use of Bins, Robe Hooks, or Baskets

The purpose of the bins, baskets, or robe hooks is to provide additional storage. The clothing items that go into these storage spaces are those that you can wear at least twice before you need to wash. Creating special storage for these clothes prevents wrinkling, separates them from the clean clothes in the closet, and reduces closet clutter.

Your Quick Start Action Step:

Folding clothes in a neat stack is an excellent way to minimize clutter in your closets. You should also hang clothes by their length to make them easy to access and to give a clear view of what you have in the closet.

Try to separate clothing that can move to a different storage space such as coats and hats.

Chapter 9:
Storage Room

Chapter 9: Storage Room

A storage room is usually one of the most challenging places to declutter in the home. It is the room where we stuff all the various items that we don't plan on using anytime soon, those that have lost their value, those with sentimental value, and those that we are unsure of dealing with. The things you accumulate in this room, as well as the various boxes present, make it overwhelming anytime you decide to declutter your storage room.

The overwhelming feeling that sweeps you shows the effect of turning your storage room into a dump for anything you are indecisive on. The amount of clutter in this room can sometimes be worth years of your life. Another issue with this space is that, since it is out of sight, it is usually out of mind.

There are various reasons why decluttering the storage space in your home is crucial. These are some of the reasons you should consider:

It Lifts a Burden Off Your Shoulders

The problem with clutter is that it often affects you mentally. The idea that you don't think about clutter if you don't see it doesn't necessarily mean that you are free from the problems the clutter creates. A storage space that is packed full prevents you from moving items from other areas of the home into the storage room.

Since there is no other storage space available, clutter steadily builds up inside the home. The physical clutter that forms also creates a mental clutter anytime you start considering how many possessions you have accumulated and the need to rid your house of clutter. Mental clutter can also develop anytime you have to think of where you may have kept an item.

You Understand That More Storage Space is Not the Solution You Require

Your desire for more storage space will increase every time you consider the amount of clutter in your home. You easily overlook the fact that it is possible to fill up as many storage spaces as possible without getting rid of clutter.

Decluttering helps you find the things you don't like or need so you can eliminate them from the home to create room for those that are required. After the decluttering process, it is easy to learn that if you limit your possessions to those things that you need, you will have enough storage space in the home to hold the items.

This effort prevents additional expenses you can incur due to renovations or moving to a bigger house.

Steps to Take in Decluttering Your Storage Room

1. Perform a Quick Surface Decluttering

    Surface decluttering doesn't require as much time and effort as deep purge decluttering. In this case, you are merely looking for the items lying around the storage room that you can throw in the trash without giving it a second thought. These include those that are broken and those without any value, both sentimental and monetary value.

If you are feeling overwhelmed by the amount of clutter in the storage space, this is a great way to start. It is much better if you focus on starting with the small items during this step. As soon as you clear out these small items, you can then work your way up through the larger pieces. Broken sports equipment and furniture can go for repairs and then to a donation center, or you can sell them.

The larger the size of the item you remove, the more space you create and the easier it becomes to work in the room.

2. Create Clutter Piles to Classify Items with Similar Functions

Your storage room will contain lots of items with different functions and uses. Amid these items, you are sure to find several items offering similar features. These are items you separate into one pile.

The reason for creating a pile is to find out which items you need to discard based on their number. If you find out you have several cartons filled with dishes you received as gifts or extras from a set, you should donate the excess to people that will appreciate them more. No matter the number of individuals living in your home, you should only require dishes that can cater for two day's worth of meals. Piling up unwashed dishes for more than two days in itself is an unhealthy habit.

All your duplicate items should be given out, including your extra hammers, bags, pans, and so on. Upon classification of these items, you will also find those that don't match your contemporary lifestyle. Let go of these items. You may find your hiking backpacks and boots lying around, but if you have no intention of taking a hike for a long time, you can donate or sell these items.

3. Guide Your Decisions Using Decluttering Questions

The major questions that help with the

decluttering process are as follows:

- Do I love this item?
- When was the last time I used this item?
- Is there a reason for having more than one of these items?

These are just some basic questions that can be of immense help while decluttering. Some individuals often fail to understand that once an item has been in the storage room for a few months without the need to use it, it is time to dispose of it. This failure makes the decluttering process difficult.

If you develop a form of discipline while decluttering, you can stick to making the right decisions based on the answers you give to the above questions concerning an object. Some items are not worth the time it takes to move them into storage or the storage space they take up.

4. Ruthlessness is a Crucial Skill for

Decluttering

Sentiments will get in the way of decluttering if you fail to develop a ruthless side. Considering the cost of purchasing a particular object can prevent you from throwing it out despite it being useless. Being ruthless makes all these irrelevant.

If you decide that all items that are of no use both now and in the future must be eliminated from the home, ruthlessness allows you to follow this decision through until the end. When decluttering some rooms in the house, you have some items that go into the "maybe box'." These are items that usually fill up the storage space.

This approach is why you no longer have room for indecision when you get to decluttering your storage space. Check the different labels on the boxes. If some have been in the storage space for over six months, or over a year for seasonal items, it is time to dispose of the items in the box.

If you think the need for an item will still crop up in the future, you should consider ridding the home of those that can be purchased at a very affordable price and within a 20-minute time duration. You should also find those that you can rent when you need them to work.

5. Items With Sentimental Value

   These are objects that you love, those you received from a loved one who has passed away or those that trigger a particular memory. Sentimental items can be a challenge to declutter and to address this issue. There will be an in-depth discussion in a later chapter.

6. Keep Your Possessions in Check by Imposing Space Restrictions

   Categorizing items has a lot of benefits when you decide to declutter. The benefits that this action offers include a quick look at how many items you have in a particular category and the ease of organizing similar items in a specific location.

When you decide to organize similar items in a specific location, it provides the opportunity to limit the amount of space you allocate to these items. Your storage space is going to be split into several sections to cover all the things you intend to keep.

By allocating space, it becomes easy to determine when you are accumulating more of a particular category without making use of the items you already have. If you are disciplined in your approach, you will see to it that these items do not extend past the allocated space by getting rid of some things.

The limit you impose on each category depends on the size of the storage room.

7. Don't Rush the Process

Once you start rushing the decluttering process, you end up letting objects without value back into the home. It is a much better option to perform the decluttering process over a few days rather than rushing it with unsatisfactory results.

Make sure that each item you take out of the storage space is carefully considered before gaining access back inside.

8. Make Sure You Properly Arrange the Storage Space After decluttering

Now you have completed the process of decluttering; the next step is to make sure that you put the storage space in order. By carefully organizing the storage space, you can further reduce the visual clutter that is caused by disorganization.

As mentioned earlier, create sections for each category of items in the storage space. You can then add a label to indicate the category that occupies a particular area. Your organization of the space should ensure that access to items in the storage space is effortless. This outcome will reduce your stress anytime you have to come to search for something.

Your Quick Start Action Step:

If you want to see tangible results in large areas like your storage spaces, dedicate specific days to check the maybe boxes. These are boxes of items you are unsure of their fate. Getting rid of those that have been there for over six months without being touched can free up space in the storage.

Create a reminder by including the date on which it will be exactly six months after taking a maybe box to your storage room.

You can also get rid of old equipment and electronics on this date.

Chapter 10: Entryways, Mudrooms, and Foyers

Chapter 10: Entryways, Mudrooms, and Foyers

The entryway, mudroom, or foyer is a part of the house whose primary purpose is to store objects that we take out daily and to connect the outside of the house to the inside. The entryway is quite easy to identify with its linoleum flooring and the inclusion of a coat closet.

A mudroom is quite similar to the entryway except it doesn't appear in all homes. This area makes it more of a secondary, less important entryway. Nonetheless, it is quite useful in the storage of shoes, wet clothing, outerwear, and footwear to ensure the cleanliness of the home's interior.

Depending on the design of the house, the entryway can vary from a very spacious one to a minimal space. Due to the high traffic through this area of the home, it must remain clutter-free. Decorations are of minor concern in the entryway.

The other purpose that makes the entryway an

essential part of the home is that it offers storage spaces. These are spaces where visitors and members of the family can keep their stuff for the duration they will be inside and easily pick it up when it is time to leave.

There are various things you want your entryway or mudroom to hold. These are the things that visitors and family members frequently carry into the home on their way in. Some of the items you should create space for in the entryway include the following:

- Different types of bags such as the briefcases, school bags, purses, backpacks, and gym bags
- Jackets and coats
- Your mail
- Shoes
- Umbrellas, hats, scarves, gloves and other weather-related clothing or accessories
- Electronics, coins, keys, cellphones, and other items in the pockets of an individual

There are various reasons why you should consider having a clutter-free entryway in the home. It makes it easy to find your essential possessions as you head out for the day. However, that isn't the only reason you should keep this area clutter-free. Read on to the next section to find out more.

Why it is Important to Declutter Your Entryway

There are some simple reasons why you should put in extra effort to declutter this space in the home. Some of these essential reasons include:

To Prevent Frustration

When the entryway is cluttered, it becomes challenging to find the items you need to get to work. It becomes annoying if you have to search through numerous things for your essential possessions like shoes, a briefcase, or umbrella under a pile of clutter. Your frustration builds up due to the unnecessary items you keep seeing as you continue your search.

To Avoid Embarrassment

Neighbors and friends are guests that you will need to entertain sooner or later. The entryway is the first place that these guests enter when visiting your home. The first impression that guests get out of a cluttered entryway lowers their expectations for your home. It is an embarrassing situation to have your friends see your house full of clutter.

You Waste Less Time

Your morning routine might involve getting dressed in your room and then moving to the entryway to complete your preparation for work. This preparation will include taking out your shoes, outerwear, and bag. If there is lots of clutter covering the area, it becomes difficult to take what you need.

You waste more time searching for these items, and you often leave home late. Removing clutter in this area saves you time when preparing for work.

Steps to Take in Decluttering

1. Discard Non-essential Items

    Typical clutter that takes space in the entryway and mudroom includes broken umbrellas, work boots with soles peeled off, old coats no longer in use, and other damaged items. Take time to remove these items that create clutter in the entryway.

2. Place a Trash Bin Close By

   If there is a trash bin close to the entryway, it makes it easier to dispose of your waste when stepping into the house or heading out. This placement can be useful if you want to immediately get rid of junk mail before it makes its way into the home to create paper clutter.

3. Restrict the Items That Should Be in This Space

   To ensure that you minimize clutter in the entryway or the mudroom, it is vital you make a home rule to restrict the items that are stored here. This guideline may involve limiting the number of shoes per individual, separating objects that are better off in another storage space or controlling the number of hats or coats you hang by the door. By imposing this restriction, you can prevent members of your family from creating a mess anytime they come in.

4. Make Use of Baskets

   Cane or wicker baskets not only offer great aesthetics, but they are also an excellent form of storage. You can decide on the number of baskets that should be in the entryway or mudroom depending on the needs of your home. Use the baskets in sorting and organizing any item that will stay in the entryway or mudroom.

5. Store Objects on the Wall

   Decluttering is about making sure there is a storage space for different items. To create more storage space in your entryway, look towards the wall to properly utilize the vertical space available. You can make use of labeled tags or fancy hooks to store umbrellas, bags, and coats with ease. This implementation makes them easily accessible when making your way out of the house.

6. Install Small Cupboards

Cabinets or cupboards in the entryway can be useful if they have several drawers installed. They occupy minimal entryway space but offer a reasonable amount of storage. The idea of selecting a small cupboard is to provide a restriction on the number of items that make their way into the cabinets. To make more productive use of the cupboard, each drawer can have a label to indicate the objects that go into a specific drawer.

Your Quick Start Action Step:

Broken umbrellas, shoes caked in mud, and old work boots are items that can easily be discarded from this area. If you don't have any, you can install hooks on the wall to make room for coats and hats.

Chapter 11: Home Office

Chapter 11: Home Office

The home office is a room where you get work done. This area may be used for your business, a project, or any task you take home from the office. It is the one room where you can improve your productivity and focus.

It is common to find clutter in this room, and there are simple steps you can take to declutter.

Decluttering the Home Office

1. Don't Mix Business and Pleasure

   Having a section of your home double as your office isn't a bad idea. But you've got to keep it organized. Taking off anything that does not relate to your work is a great way to decongest the desk and clear off all items not suitably placed. You pay deductibles to the Internal Revenue Service if the home office is used exclusively for business purposes. However, you can avoid this deductible if you try to create another role for the office, maybe by also using it as a guest room. But, you should separate your business room from your leisure room by attending to your guests or working on your crafts in a different location.

2. Go Through Paper Items

Usually, the office is home to different clutter, including relevant documents and trash. It is there you find piles of bills, documents, receipts, invoices, and other pieces of paper. The task of ensuring a less muddled office becomes easier once you start clearing off the paper. Doing this begins with sorting the different pieces of paper into sections in order of importance. We can sort them into Files, To-do, and Junk. In that way, you can do your cabinet filing properly, shred, and trash the junk pile. The To-do pile can remain in a basket next to your desk to remind yourself of the files that need urgent attention.

Let us examine some of the tips to help you remove clutter from your home office:

- Scan all relevant documents, invoices, and receipts. Make a digital record of the papers.
- Try to shred all the paper you won't need anymore.
- Store older files in a plastic bin and keep them away from the office space. You can store them in the basement, garage, or you create a space for them, but let it be outside the office.
- Set aside a particular space for vital mail, paper, or documents that need urgent attention.
- Ensure circular files are appropriately filed when you're doing your filing paperwork.

3. Clear Off Your Desk

The desk is not a storeroom, so try as much as possible to take away all papers and documents that should be in the cabinet or drawers. Only keep items that you use frequently or that need urgent action on the desk. Never allow any food or oil close to the desk, computer, table lamp, or other desk essentials. Make optimal use of the office drawers. You can keep a few embellishments on the desk, but don't add so many you reduce the desk's functionality.

4. Clean Out and Organize Drawers

   Take regular cleaning of the drawers and office cabinets seriously. The drawers shouldn't look like piles of junk when you open them. There are three simple steps you can take to take care of your office supplies:

5. Empty the Office Drawers

   The first action is to take everything out of the drawers. Just as the desk is not meant for unimportant and non-urgent items and documents, the drawers are also not meant to keep papers that will not be needed for over a year. Take away documents that you have not used for (six) months. If there is a necessity to keep these files in the office, you can buy small boxes or containers to keep them. Arrange files in such a way that like-items stay near each other. This step will help you avoid a free-floating of objects in the drawers.

6. Pruning Files

While it is often recommended that you keep files and papers for some time before you discard them, it is also imperative to section these files to avoid disorganized drawers. Take time at least once every six months to check these files. Put them into sections of current files, archival files, and obsolete files. Move the archival files to a box that you have clearly labeled. Get rid of the old files.

7. Invest in a Shredder

Do not discard papers, documents, and files carelessly. Be careful with paper that carries your name, signature, and personal or official identity, including bank account, legal agreement, etc. Shredding them before discarding them will help you reduce the risk of identity theft. Purchase some shredders and a wastebasket and put them within reach to be sure that your documents are adequately shredded and disposed of.

8. Tame Your Cords

The crisp, fantastic look you want for your home office desk can be achieved only if you ensure that you wrangle in your cords. Keep the essential in the home office. Try to go online and search for a couple of cord management products that are used to tie up and tame cords. Below are a few of cord hacks you can use:

- Try to label cords with tape. With this, it becomes easier to tell what cable goes with each device.
- Hold cords that are co unplugged up on your desk with binder clips.
- Use twist-ties or rubber bands to tie up excess cables.

9. Create a Printing Station

   Never cluster old and in-use printers in one place. Designate a space in the office for your printer and printer supplies. Wireless printers don't need to stay on the desk. Place them in a cabinet or create a space for them in the office.

10. Create a Mail Station

    Mail is the most likely paper to come into the office, and you will need to stay in control to keep it from accumulating. Try to create a mail station by making a folder for incoming and outgoing mail. Also, make a folder for every family member. As soon as the mail comes in, quickly file it in the mail station.

11. Use Office Organizers for Clutter Control

    Partition office supplies into various sections. You can do this by organizing items of similar purpose in the same place while 'unlike' items are placed separately. You can keep stationery together and papers in another section. Again, try to store all mail supplies in one drawer, and so on. In this way, you won't have the stress of ransacking the entire box or cabinet of files while searching for one file, thus ending up disorganizing the whole place. Meanwhile, if your storage and space are limited, try to use the vertical arrangement method.

Installing shelves on the wall is a great idea that will help create enough space for your items and documents. Shelving will also give you room to arrange your files, books, work manuals, and materials in a place you can easily have access to them. It also helps you with hanging filing systems and lots more. Never leave the shelves hanging without support. To achieve a perfect result, try to stage shelves with pretty office organizers such as hanging wire baskets, bins, drawers, boxes, etc. Floating shelves are not suitable for large rooms, so only use them in relatively small rooms. The reason for this is that floating shelves don't demand corbels or brackets for their installation. Try to reduce the clutter on your home office desk to 20% covered or less. Use a tall armoire in your office as it gives a ton of additional storage opportunities where you can stash your wireless printer. Never dump junk items on your desk.

Your Quick Start Action Step:

Take time every day to shred any junk mail or document with information that shouldn't be exposed. If you don't have a shredder, invest in one as soon as you can. Clear your desk of any clutter as soon as you are through with work for the day.

Chapter 12: Basement and Attic

Chapter 12: Basement and Attic

The attic and basement are two storage spaces that are found in the home. While the basement is usually below the ground floor in the house, you can expect to see the attic directly below the roof. The use of attics and basements as storage areas is usually due to the difficulty accessing these areas as well as the lack of comfort due to their design. Despite these issues, you can still find some of these spaces converted into a room or office in several homes.

As storage spaces, the attic and basement are places where you load items you are sure you won't need for a long time, those that you keep for sentimental value, outdated products, and things that you haven't decided what to do with. The selections of items that go into these spaces usually create clutter in the rooms. Your inability to discard these items means you keep stuffing these items until you run out of space.

When it is time to declutter these storage spaces, don't kid yourself into thinking you can complete the decluttering in a few hours. You need to dedicate a few days to decluttering an attic or basement.

The strategy you apply in this room is the divide and conquer strategy. By separating the room into zones, you can choose a zone to focus on first before moving on to the next area. This strategy eases your workload and makes the process less overwhelming.

Steps to Declutter Your Basement or Attic

1. Split your Attic or Basement into Various Segments

    First, segment attic and basement organization into six easy steps. With this, you can declutter your basement without feeling stressed out.

    To make work in your basement easy, you should take it one section at a time. Get started by working on a stack of boxes, kid's toys, and clothes that are no longer in use, periodic decorations and shelves.

    While working in a particular segment, take time to complete that segment before moving on to another. If you are focusing on bins, ensure that all bins are emptied. If shelves are what you want to focus on first, ensure they are cleared completely. It will be very distracting to start working on another segment when you are not done with the previous section.

2. Everything Should Be Sorted Into Bins

Since you are focused on an area in your basement that is used in storing stuff, it is okay to take out one bin and concentrate your attention there to either dispose of the items you come across or holding on to them. While at this, if you come across anything that you think can be fixed without you having to spend too much, it is okay to have a different pile for such items. To make sure that you end up fixing such things, it is vital that you set a deadline. If the deadline comes and goes before you fix them, you should go ahead and dispose of them.

3. Take the Items You Intend to Dispose of

Out of the House

Before separating the items that you intend to keep, you should take everything that you want to dispose of out of your house. Once outside ensure that they are all kept in the trash bin. If you do not intend to throw them away but plan to donate them, you should move them straight into the vehicle that you will use to move them away from your house. If you are not donating them immediately, it is okay to keep them in your garage for a while.

4. Keep Items That Are Alike in One Piece

The same tips that can help you organize your bathroom can be applied when getting your basement decluttered. Keeping similar items in one pace will make it very easy for you to have access to them whenever you need them. Are you in possession of ornaments that can be used to decorate trees? If yes, you should then keep decorations of similar colors together. By doing this, when next you want to decorate a tree, there will be no need to get out all the boxes with ornaments, you can pick the color you want.

5. Ensure Bins and Boxes Are Labeled

While putting already sorted out items back into bins and boxes, you must label all the things you are putting into the boxes. If you don't want to write on the bin, it is okay to have a list of the contents of the container written on a piece of paper and then paste it on the bin. This way, you can know the contents without opening it. Another way to do this is to make use of a label maker to put removable but semi-permanent labels on the bin. It is easier to have an idea of what is inside if you make use of clear bins.

Your Quick Start Action Step:

The quick action step here is similar to your other storage spaces. Take out old junk that is not going to be needed anytime soon.

Chapter 13: Books and Paper Documents

Chapter 13: Books and Paper Documents

Books and paper documents easily create clutter in the home. Paper tends to scatter around due to their lightweight and possibly clutter the house. The zeal to gather information and learn more about a topic make books a necessity in the home. Unfortunately, having a lot of books could also lead to clutter.

These books and paper documents need to be decluttered regularly. Otherwise, they would quickly gather in the home if you're not careful.

Getting Books and Paper Documents Decluttered

1. Arrange Your Books or Documents in Different Categories

   To successfully declutter your books and other paper documents, it is essential you know exactly what you have. You can achieve this by bringing all these items out of their hiding spots and then placing them in front of you. You can then separate them into different categories.

Categorizing the books and paper documents is an essential step for those that consider themselves book lovers. However, the number of books you have will be impossible to declutter in one sitting. The categories you can split these items into include:

- Magazines
- Visual books (art books, coffee table books, etc.)
- General books (books you read for fun)
- Children's books
- Practical books (reference books, cookbooks, etc.)

2. Identify the Books That Get Your Heart Racing

To make the process very useful, it is best to treat all your books as if you intend to dispose of all of them. Give each book an equal chance of being kept by looking through all of them and then coming up with a decision on the books that you intend to continue reading.

While trying to sort out books, Marie Kondo has made it known to her students that it is best they do not go on to read these books while they are still being handled and thinking of the books to keep. The reason is that going this route will end up making the entire process never-ending. It will also make it a lot more challenging to choose which books should be kept and which books should be disposed of.

What if you suddenly think to yourself, "I may like to reread it another time."

One major challenge many people face when disposing of books is the thought that a day will come when they would like to read the same book over again. This mindset makes it difficult to discard the books that you should dispose of.

To people facing the challenge of wanting to read a book sometime later, it is possible you never really want to read the book. You rarely find people that pick up books that have been on the shelf for a period and go through them or read them a second time if they have read them before. And due to this, there is nothing wrong in disposing of a book you intend to read later.

It is a better option to read a book the first time you come across it as that is the best time to do so. If you are unable to read a book the first time you get ahold of it, the chance that you would read it another time is very slim.

Nothing is absolute, and some people are exceptions to this statement.

Sometimes, you will notice that you are longing for a book that you have recently donated. In this case, a more suitable option is to look for an electronic copy of the book. The information is usually the same, although some people say they prefer reading the physical copy of a book.

3. Those That Don't Get Your Heart Racing Should be Discarded

There are certain books you read that get your heart racing and make you ponder what will happen next. Then there are those that you struggle to get to the end. There is a vast difference between these books. Those that get your heart racing are the books you are likely to read again. For the second group, you would be doing yourself a favor by disposing of them.

There are different ways to dispose of books. You can try giving them to a church or the neighborhood library. The Amazon FBA program offers an opportunity for individuals to sell off their books with ease. Also, you often experience a form of pleasure anytime you dispose of some of your books to eliminate clutter and create space.

4. Arrange the Leftover Books Properly

As soon as we have taken out all the books that we were not excited about, the next step is to reorganize those that are left in the home. Since you already separated them based on categories, you should do the same when organizing them back onto the shelves. Avoid stacking the books when arranging as this makes it easier for them to fall off.

If you have excess space, then mixing between stacking and standing the books can help close up the spaces between books to prevent them from falling off. Only in situations like this should you consider stacking books.

Questions to Ask to Make Decluttering Easier

Have I gone through the book? Is it one I would love to sit down to read another time?

Do you have a book that you have already read once and do not have any plans to reread it? If yes, then there is no need to keep the book as it is now of no purpose on your shelf. More often than not, novels fall into this group. The only exceptions are when these novels contain some life-transforming stories that you might want to go through a couple more times.

Do you have a book that you are yet to go through? Do you have any plans to read it tomorrow or the day after? If going through this book is not something you are excited about; it is best to give it up. There are lots of books in the world, and you will only have the opportunity to read a handful of these books throughout your life. So, if you have a book you think you will not read, you should not let it occupy space.

Do you use the book frequently?

If you have to always refer to a book, you should not dispose of it. It still meets a pressing need and should be kept.

Is it an extra copy?

Having multiple copies of the same book in your home library might seem funny. But it is possible. You might not believe you have duplicates in your library until you double check, such as finding a paperback version before realizing that you also have a hardcover version of the same book.

Are you sentimental about the book?

You should not hold on to a book out of sentiment. A lot of times, we keep books that we do not need because they came as gifts. If you have a book that is of no use, you should ask yourself if you would keep such a book if it were not a gift.

What are the reasons I am keeping this book?

This is a question you should ask yourself. A lot of people keep their old books for the appearance it gives the home. The truth is even if you dispose of those unwanted books, your home will still look good and even better space-wise.

Is the book available at the library?

Libraries contain a lot more books than you have in your home. If you can get a book at the library, it is okay to let it go.

Is the magazine or book outdated?

Trying to keep books that don't hold relevant information can be quite straightforward to deal with. This scenario can include keeping old travel guides, textbooks, and magazines. A lot of people have unintentionally continued holding on to magazines that promoted trends that are now outdated. This is in addition to keeping travel guides that advertise places that no one would want to visit anymore. The truth remains that a lot of the fantastic restaurants that you would have loved to visit about three decades ago are no longer what they used to be. So, one question you have to ask yourself is, "Are the many magazines I have in my possession still important? Can their contents still be beneficial to me?" If your answer is no, then, you do not need them.

Will these books be important to someone else?

Realizing that others would benefit greatly from a book that you are still holding on to will make it easier to dispose of. It is a lot better to release a book that you are sure will only make your shelf look better if others benefit significantly from it.

Your Quick Start Action Step:

Simply returning books to shelves and arranging magazines back into the magazine racks can quickly remove clutter from a space. Add it to your schedule to organize books and documents.

Chapter 14:
Garage

Chapter 14: Garage

The garage used to be nothing more than a space for parking cars, keeping your motorcycles, and storing bicycles. As years roll by, this area of the home has become very important in the lives of many individuals.

There are lots of reasons why the garage remains a crucial space in most homes. For most men, they get the opportunity to flex their creativity when they spend time in their garage. It is from this space that furniture and DIY projects come to life. It is how they create memories.

Besides creating personal memories, it is also a great place to create memories with the kids. You get to bond as you both struggle to paint a cupboard, fix a bicycle tire, build a new dog house, and many more activities.

In addition to the fun activities you can engage in, the garage also offers room for anything that needs to be stored. Tools, a workbench, bicycle racks, lawnmowers, and many more are easily accessible when stored in this space. You can create a mess without considering the implications.

The lack of implications is usually what leads to clutter in the garage. Flexing your creativity gives room for incomplete projects to make a home in the garage. The opportunity to store anything in the garage also gives you the freedom to leave items from ten years ago laying around.

To address the clutter in the garage, the divide and conquer strategy is most effective. You don't have the luxury of selecting what items move to better storage since this is usually where you move things you are indecisive about. The decluttering process involves being ruthless in letting go of useless items.

Steps to Declutter the Garage

The steps you take to declutter should involve paying attention to specific groups of similar items that commonly cause garage clutter. In this section, the steps given relate to many of the everyday objects you find in the garage.

1. Suspend Bicycles on the Wall or Racks

   The garage offers great storage space for bicycles in the home. You must create a room to store them properly. Whatever storage space you create for storing bikes should not impede traffic through the garage.

   You can purchase a bicycle rack at a closet accessory store or bicycle shop. Make sure you get one that is sturdy and durable. Depending on the design you select, you can also get baskets or shelves for keeping water bottles, gloves, helmets, and other biking gear. Use screws in fastening the bicycle gear to a wall in the garage.

   Another option is to visit a hardware store to buy clips that you can use in suspending the bicycles from the wall.

2. Store Your Athletic Gear Properly

   Depending on the sports gear you want to store, you can purchase shelves or racks specially designed to suit your needs.

Walk into any closet accessories shop or home center to find shelves that meet your specifications.

You can also put your creativity to work by designing a storage device for sports equipment at a much cheaper cost. The various sports equipment that should go into the shelves, racks, or DIY storage devices include soccer balls, golf clubs, baseball bats, skis, tennis rackets, and in-line skates.

For your protective gear, you can install hooks or shelves close to the garage entrance so that they are easy easily accessible and visible to anyone that needs them.

3. Purchase Wheeled Storage

These are for sports gear and camping equipment that you will be loading into your car frequently. Instead of letting them occupy space close to the vehicle, put them in wheeled storage that is easy to move around. Doing so makes it suitable for easing the stress of loading and unloading items.

4. Purchase a Fold-down Table

   Your repair activities will be challenging unless you have a table to use. The garage is a great place to perform these repairs and also store the table. You must get a table that you can fold to ensure that traffic space in the garage remains free since it can align vertically with the wall.

   You can open the table and lock it in place horizontally anytime you need it for work.

5. Discard Old Catalogs, Magazines, and Newspapers

   Once any of these items find its way into the garage, it means it is no longer of use to anyone in the home. You should dispose of these items to rid your garage of the clutter they create. If this is a challenge, then start by keeping special editions while disposing of the rest.

6. You Don't Need Those Old Electronics

The garage is an excellent place to store things you want to keep out of sight. These include your old electronics like your fax machine, computers, and printers. If these items are far behind what current technology offers, then you should decide to let go of these items. Donating these items may not be easy, but you are sure to find a recycling program that will accept these items.

7. Tools

The tools you keep in the garage are often a considerable part of the clutter in this storage space. The first set of tools you should go after are those that are broken. If it has been sitting on the shelf for over six months without getting repaired, then you don't need it anymore. Throw these tools out of the home.

You should also check for tools that serve as duplicates and dispose of the excess. You may purchase different toolsets and find specific items that you already own.

Keeping five hammers or band hack saws isn't an excellent idea for creating a clutter-free garage.

8. Paint Cans

The reason why you probably have a lot of paint cans in your garage is due to the long shelf life of the contents. Paint can stay good for as long as ten years if you don't open the containers while those that have been used at one point can still last as long as five years. It is common for individuals to decide to keep the leftover paint from a home improvement project.

Depending on how long the paint cans have been in your garage, it may finally be time to let them go. Drop the cans at a waste disposal close by or find out programs concerning paint recycling near you.

9. Leftover Materials

Paint cans are just a part of the leftover clutter from a home improvement project that you are holding on to. There are other materials like paint trays and brushes as well as DIY tools that you are keeping around. Unless there is an upcoming project you have in mind, you should dispose of these items. You are likely going to purchase new tools before remembering you have some old tools when planning for another project anyway.

10. Old Forms of Entertainment

DVDs, CDs, and Online Streaming are just some of the current options available for your entertainment. Besides these options, there was a time when your home entertainment was dependent on cassette tapes, VHS tapes, a VCR, and tape players. Well, that time is past, and no one would enjoy going through the trouble of flipping to the B-Side to see the end of a movie.

If these tapes are collections of old albums or movies, you can start searching for them in digital formats. As soon as you get the digital formats, you can start getting rid of the physical copies.

11. Décor

Many forms of home décor make up garage clutter. It may merely be some holiday decorations that are no longer in vogue. Others may be an old chair that needs the fabric changed. If you have forgotten about these items, then you can start thinking of how to push them out of the house finally. Thrift stores can help with this or take them to a donation center.

Your Quick Start Action Step:

Remove all the work tools laying around, arrange them in a toolbox, or hang them on hooks on the wall. Simply putting bicycles on their racks and clearing them off the pathway can make the garage seem clutter-free.

Chapter 15: Dealing with Items You Love

Chapter 15: Dealing with Items You Love

Watching your kids grow or losing a loved one are some of the most emotional events in our lives. There is an indescribable joy that you experience when you see your kid take his first step or bring home a drawing of the family during the kindergarten years. These experiences slowly become memories, and the only way to recall these memories is to take a look at an item that is connected to them.

The same applies to the loss of a loved one. Despite the sorrow that it may bring to you, we often hold on to the possessions of a loved one to ensure that we remember them and keep their memory alive. This process is also an essential part of moving on and accepting what has happened.

So, what happens when you need to discard something that you hold dear in your heart? The emotional attachment we have to these items makes them challenging to discard. These items are what we refer to as those with sentimental value.

Decluttering is a challenging process that involves getting rid of a lot of things in the home. These include your clothes, electronics, shoes, and many more. The difficulty of the decluttering process multiplies anytime individuals come across such sentimental items. They are very hard to let go since they spark certain emotions and memories.

Deciding to keep these items is the usual path that people take. The problem with this choice is the simple truth that you are creating clutter in the home. Understanding that letting go is the only way to move on from the past and experience the joy of the present will help in living a better life.

If you are still in this situation and finding it difficult to let go of items of sentimental value, then it is time to find the best solutions. This chapter will assist in finding excellent ways to address the issue of sentimental clutter in your home.

Decluttering Items of Sentimental Value

1. Identify Items of Actual Value

    In decluttering items of sentimental value, you are stuck with objects that you associate with memories and those that you are fond of. You can simplify the decluttering process by discarding items that you have associated with a particular memory or individual. Without these items, you can still recollect the memories as well as various features of the individual in question.

    The items that you are fond of are those that are of real value to you. Objects in this category don't make up the clutter in your home.

2. Avoid Being Overwhelmed by Gifts

    A lot of items that are on display on most walls and shelves in the home are gifts you received from various individuals. The idea that the person that presents these gifts wants to see it any time they visit makes it difficult to declutter. It is an unnecessary obligation you create that prevents you from ridding your home of clutter.

Adopt a new approach to how you handle gifts. Once you receive it, how you use it is entirely up to you.

3. Don't Let Guilt Determine What Items You Keep

Sentiments often feed off various emotions. Guilt is one of the feelings that boosts the sentimental value of certain items. Any object you intend to keep for its sentimental value should be out of nostalgia or love.

You should understand that feeling a profound sense of guilt about a past relationship or situation won't make things right.

4. Create Digital Memories

Sentimental objects come in different

forms. The furniture from your parents' home, your children's old toys, high school pictures, and old documents make up objects of sentimental value. Regardless of the method you adopt, if you physically store them, you end up creating clutter in your storage spaces.

If you are sure no one is going to make good use of the furniture or toys you are holding on to, take a picture of the furniture or make a digital copy of your kids playing with the toys. From the pictures, you can tell the appearance of an object and recollect its physical features.

Documents and other files can be converted to a digital copy by scanning. You can then get rid of the paper clutter by shredding and disposing of it properly.

5. Learn How to Handle Clutter Created by Others

You may have excellent minimalist habits that allow you to live a clutter-free life. These habits may not necessarily align with those of your partner, roommate, or family members. In this case, you need to find a smart way to get what you want.

The famous phrase/proverb, out of sight, out of mind, has a massive impact on this situation. You and the other individual can agree on a room that they can stuff with all these items. Whatever goes on in this room is not your business.

If space is not an option, then you both need to come to an understanding. You let them put essential items on display while the others are either sold or donated. If you are lucky, merely engaging in the decluttering of your sentimental items will rub off on your partner.

6. Some Items NEED to be Donated

Here, we are not referring to donating clothes or shoes. What you need to donate in this case are items that are of historical or educational value. Some individuals love the idea of collecting various objects, including typewriters, vinyl records, china sets, old paintings, and more.

There is a high chance you will receive some of these items if you lose a loved one. Despite not needing these items, you will often feel a compulsion to keep them around. You will be doing a lot of good if you look for organizations that will value these items more than you do.

Old paintings, historical photos, old books, and a few other items can go to a local history museum, library, or archive. All you need to do is perform in-depth research on different organizations and the objects that are of value to them.

7. Give to a Relative

Family heirlooms fall within the category of objects with sentimental value. Despite their importance, you may have no need or interest in these items. Rather than disposing of or donating the object, it is best you give it to a relative.

Discuss with other members of your extended family to find an individual that would cherish the heirloom. It is a better alternative to putting it in storage or discarding the object.

8. One Item to Represent a Collection

    A simple solution to address sentimental clutter is to get rid of collections. Some gifts come in a selection of numerous items. Merely selecting one thing from the collection and giving out the rest is an excellent way to control clutter in the home. It remains possible to associate the memory to this item in the same manner as the entire collection.

9. Learn to Create a Scrapbook

    Creating a scrapbook is a very straightforward process. All you need is a glue stick and a notebook to begin your project. It saves space and helps retain the memories you treasure.

    Scrapbooking is a suitable option for your

pictures and paper items. Cut the crucial parts of the picture or paper and glue them to the notebook. To make it more fun and more comfortable to recollect the memories, remember to add notes and descriptions on each page.

It occupies less space and doesn't require expensive supplies to start.

How to Deal With Emotional Resistance When Decluttering

When decluttering sentimental items, it is common to find yourself in a situation where your emotions prevent you from letting go. Getting yourself out of the grip of these emotions is vital if you want to go on with the decluttering process. You need to have a plan that is useful in such situations.

Creating a plan depends on what you feel will work better for you based on your personality. Notwithstanding, here are a few steps to get you out of this situation or help you create a more elaborate plan:

- You should try to envision the joy on the face of another individual when you donate these items to those in need. When you know you can make an impact on the life of another person, it often creates a sense of comfort inside you.
- Look for something better to replace the item. This process fulfills the idea of keeping the best and getting rid of others. If you find yourself emotionally inclined to hold a birthday card from your grandmother, you can search for a handwritten letter to replace the card.
- Despite not being the physical object, keeping a digital image of a sentimental item will go a long way in easing the emotions you feel.
- If your emotional barrier seems too strong to overcome, then it is time to call in some of your friends.
- Build your resistance by letting go of sentimental items last. By decluttering with regular clutter, you develop your ability to let go.

Your Quick Start Action Step:

On your schedule, add notes to remind you that you should create digital copies of sentimental items so they become easy to dispose of in the future. You should call different organizations that will find these items useful.

Chapter 16: Decluttering in One Day

Chapter 16: Decluttering in One Day

Don't get the wrong idea; decluttering is a process that takes a lot of time to complete. That is why, in this book, each room had a specific chapter discussing how to declutter. That was the small wins strategy, and for someone just getting into the habit of decluttering that is the most effective method.

Moving on to decluttering the entire home in one day requires an in-depth understanding of the small wins strategy. The one-day decluttering process is you putting the experience and speed you have developed while implementing the small wins strategy to work. It is also highly dependent on the fact that you have recently carried out a significant decluttering process in the home.

What to Avoid When Decluttering in One-Day

The time you require to complete a decluttering process makes it challenging to create time to fit in other chores. Any day you schedule for decluttering, there are several tasks you must ensure you don't perform. These are chores closely related to the decluttering process, so it is easy to get carried away. These include the following:

Cleaning

It is common to find clutter covered in grime or dust as you declutter the home. You must ensure you avoid the temptation to clean the house until a later time. If you are sure you want to complete the decluttering process in one day, then you can't lose any time deep cleaning the home.

Organizing

Understand that, just like decluttering, organizing your possessions takes a lot of time. Trying to reorganize items while decluttering will take your focus off your original goal. Schedule a different day to organize the home after the decluttering process.

Deep Purging

The one-day decluttering process is a surface

decluttering process. It means you don't have time to spend opening all the boxes you keep in your attic or basement. If you want to perform this form of decluttering, then you should engage in the room-by-room decluttering of the home on another day.

Decluttering of Closets and Clothing

Once you set your sights on the items in your closet, you won't have any time to declutter any other area of the home that day. To avoid wasting precious time, it is best you avoid clothing and closet areas during the one-day house decluttering.

Preparation for the process

No matter how trivial it may seem, decluttering in one day requires preparation. Your preparation should extend to both the physical and mental preparation necessary for the procedure. Here are some of the steps you need to take to prepare for this day physically:

- Get boxes and label them
- Assemble the required supplies

- Timer for proper time management
- Get comfortable shoes and clothes you will wear on that day

Now that you know the things you need to prepare for the process, you must also realize that your speed matters a lot to the success of this process. You have to move quickly from one room to the other.

This goal of fast implementation is the reason for getting a timer. Set the timer to 30 minutes for each room you want to declutter. The timer will let you know when it is time to move to the next place. Assessing your progress within the 30 minutes you spent decluttering a room will help determine if you strayed from your original purpose.

A plan for how you intend to donate the items you don't need also matters. You can reach out to different organizations and thrift stores to determine the next step to take. Some of these organizations go the extra mile of coming to your doorstep to pick up the donations. For others, you can get information on how, when, and where to complete the donation.

How to Perform the One-day Decluttering

Since the process is a surface decluttering, the four-box strategy is useful for the procedure. Below is a room-by-room surface decluttering guide. The guide gives you suggestions on the items that should go into each box.

Feel free to edit and remove rooms based on your preference:

1. Dining Room

    The area you should focus on is the dining table. This approach applies if family members have turned this surface into a dump for various items. Sort items on the dining table as follows:

    - Move box: Items such as laptops that don't belong on this table but are comfortable to use.
    - Storage box: Seasonal décor, fine china, and special linens.

- Donation box: Linen you no longer need but is in good condition, unwanted dishes, and old décor designs.
- Trash: Table linens with stains, old candles, and paperwork that needs shredding.

2. Coat Closet
    - Move box: Any excess of shoes or sandals that are still in use.
    - Storage box: Shoes and outerwear that is out of season.
    - Donation box: Outerwear that is no longer wanted, those that are out of style, and those that no longer fit.
    - Trash: Broken umbrellas and other items too damaged to use.

3. Kitchen

Countertops and tables in the kitchen should be your primary focus during the one-day decluttering session. Since the kitchen is quite important, you can allocate an additional 5 minutes solely to get rid of expired food items.

- Move: Mail, family members' personal items, and appliances that shouldn't be on the countertops.
- Storage Box: Out-of-season décor, tools, and gadgets for once in a year recipes.
- Donation Box: Food items you won't use and appliances that you don't need.
- Trash: Expired food items.

4. Living Room

The living room is one of the places that quickly gathers surface clutter. You may need to declutter this room more often than the others.

- Move: Personal belongings of family members, books you intend to read, and functional toys that are creating clutter.

- Storage Box: Out-of-season décor, toys, games, books, magazines, and movies.
- Donation Box: Games, décor you no longer need, old toys, books, and movies.
- Trash: Broken toys, old magazines or newspapers, incomplete puzzle or game sets, and old coloring books.

5. Linen Closet
    - Move: Cleaning items that don't belong in this closet.
    - Storage Box: Bed linens and towels that are in a proper package but not currently in use.
    - Donation Box: Excess bath and body products you are sure you won't use, bed linens and towels you don't want.
    - Trash: Bath and body products that are expired, old bed linens or towels, old cleaning supplies, and actual waste like plastic wrappings.

6. Bathrooms
    - Move: Excess toiletries like bath/body products, towels that can go to the linen closets, and personal belongings.
    - Storage Box: Extra bath toys.
    - Donation Box: Hairstyling tools you no longer need and bath/body products that are still usable but you don't want.
    - Trash: Empty bath/body products, empty nail polish bottles, used makeup, used toilet paper rolls, soiled cleaning supplies, and broken bath toys.
7. Bedrooms

The clutter you are aiming to remove from the bedroom is those on the floor, bedside tables, and top of the dresser.

    - Move: Personal belongings that don't belong in the bedroom.
    - Storage Box: Out-of-season clothes.

- Donation Box: Bedroom décor that you are sure you don't need any longer.
- Trash: All items that should be thrown away, such as wrappers.

8. Storage Areas (Basement, Attic, Garage)

Home areas like the storage areas and clothes closet often require deep purging to declutter properly. Regardless, there are still some items you can remove from storage areas with the surface decluttering process.

Ensure you don't waste time deep purging these areas. Stick to the plan and perform a surface decluttering.

- Storage Box: Décor that will still be of use.
- Donation Box: Various items that have been in storage for over six months.
- Trash: Old newspapers, things that are broken beyond repair, product

boxes, cardboard boxes, and other old packing materials.

Your Quick Start Action Step:

Pick a free day, like Saturday or Sunday, to engage in this decluttering session. You must mentally prepare yourself for the one-day decluttering session by shifting your targets to trash and surface clutter alone. This strategy is to ensure that you can follow through with the steps listed above.

Bonus Chapter: Decluttering Before Moving

Bonus Chapter: Decluttering Before Moving

This chapter is an essential addition that will be useful when you decide to move into a new home or apartment. Decluttering is a vital process you need to engage in to ensure you have less stress and spend less when moving.

Moving companies will charge extra if you have to add the things you don't need when packing. Paying for things you know you don't want isn't a smart decision, so you need to let go of these items before the moving date arrives. You also save yourself time and stress if you have a reduced number of possessions to unpack.

Over their lifetime, the average individual will move to a new home 11.7 times. This is based on a study carried out by the United States Census Bureau. The overall population structure and age group with increased chances of relocating in a year were the two datasets used in determining this value.

The study by the United States Census Bureau

was performed in 2007 with a new study in 2014. The 2014 results were from independent research that indicated a drop in this value from 11.7 to 11.3 times.

As we have already established, decluttering is the only way to reduce the items you need to pack. The things you should focus on are the non-essentials and those that have been in your storage space for the last few months or years.

And if you wait for the last minute, then all the random things end up in boxes and garbage bags to be trucked over to the new place. It's not a pretty picture: opening the "oh what's in here?" box only to find loose change, dirty dishes, paperwork you needed last week and the shoes that disappeared during the move.

Why You Should Declutter Before a Move

There are numerous reasons why decluttering is essential before moving out of your current home. Understanding these benefits can get you into the mood to engage in the decluttering process in anticipation of this day. Some of the excellent benefits include the following:

- You save money on moving expenses.
- There are fewer items to unpack and arrange when you arrive at the new home.
- You create more space after unboxing and organizing your stuff.
- You find things that you can sell to cover a reasonable part of the moving expenses.
- Identifying things you don't need is vital and can touch the lives of others through donations.

Now that you know some of the benefits of decluttering before you move, what steps do you take to declutter?

How to Declutter Before Moving

There are steps you can take to ensure that you are making progress towards decluttering for a move. Some of the steps you should consider are given in this section:

1. Start Early

    Deciding what to pack and things that

need to be discarded isn't something you do when the moving company employees are at your doorstep. Give yourself ample time to properly declutter and get rid of the items you don't intend to take along. You should start the decluttering process a minimum of two weeks before the planned date.

You don't need to spend the entire day decluttering. Working 2-3 hours a day will help you make significant progress. Working on this short period of time is also an excellent strategy since it means that you won't get too tired and give in to the temptation of stuffing boxes randomly just to finish the task quickly.

2. Start Using Excesses

Shampoo, toilet paper, toiletries as well as other household goods that you purchase in large quantities should be used. If you start using them, it steadily reduces the stockpile of products you need to take with you when moving. It will be a good thing if you start running out of these items. You can then choose to buy small packages of these items if you need to.

3. Implement the Four-box Strategy

Following the explanation of this strategy in chapter 5, you take three boxes and a trash can into each room you intend to declutter. Check through the entire room, empty the drawers and closets, check underneath the beds, and examine the shelves for the different items you need to declutter.

Each item goes into one of the three boxes or the trash. One box should contain the items you intend to sell or donate, another for those that you intend to keep, and the last box for those that are moving to a different room.

4. Discard Expired Products

Go through the items in your bathroom cupboards and in your pantry to identify those that are past their expiration dates.

If you are not sure of the expiry dates of certain items like spices, try to recall exactly when you bought the item.

Some spices can last several years. If you take in the scent and it seems like it has lost its potency, then you can throw it out. Foodstuffs in your refrigerator should also be checked to determine if they should be discarded.

Other items like makeup products that are still useful despite their age should still be considered. Those that you have had for years without making use of them should be discarded immediately.

5. Decide on How to Donate or Sell Items

In Chapter 3 of this book, you learned some of the best ways to donate specific items. Giving up an item to charity not only lifts a huge burden from your home, but it also makes you feel better about yourself. You also need to consider the things that you want to sell.

Hosting a garage sale may seem like a good idea, but it isn't the best alternative. In most cases, it requires a lot of energy and robs you of valuable time. It is quite common to have a low turnout with meager profits from these sales. To save yourself the trouble, visit an online platform like Craigslist to sell off some of these items quickly.

6. Use the Opportunity to Get Rid of Excess Toys

    Your kids' toys may occupy considerable storage space in the home, so you need to use any opportunity to declutter to your advantage. A creative way to snuff out the irrelevant toys in the house is to get them to pick out 10 – 15 toys that they want to play with as you pack your possessions. If towards the move or after moving they are still content with just these toys, then you can donate the packed items.

7. The Last Things You Should Declutter Are Those of Sentimental Value

You are preparing to move to another home, and the last thing you want to is to be overwhelmed by the emotions attached to sentimental items. Decluttering these items should come last on your list. Besides the feelings they cause to resurface, sentimental objects also cause time wastage due to indecision.

The sentimental items that you should consider discarding are those that you hide in a box in your storage room and those not on display. Most objects of sentimental value that you treasure are those that you put on display. These are the items you want to see daily.

Disposing objects of sentimental value is not a bad thing since it doesn't necessarily mean that you lose the memory connected with the object. One of the options available to you is the creation of a digital copy of the item. Take a picture, and you are all set.

Donating these items should be your

priority. Ensure you find someone that will appreciate the value of the objects you are giving out. If an item causes pain and evokes emotions of sadness, then you really shouldn't be holding on to it. If there is no benefit to holding on to an item and it has no use in the home, then discard it.

Only items that make you smile and those that can be used offer enough value to remain with you.

8. Create Time Each Day to Rest

Starting early gives you a lot of time to declutter before moving to a new place. Despite starting early, you need to limit the time you spend decluttering. This is because the process is exhausting physically, emotionally, and mentally.

After decluttering for the day, take time to recharge by having a conversation with friends or family, reading a book, or taking a cup of tea. Setting up this reward before you start decluttering for the day will provide a form of motivation to work.

9. Pack a Box of Necessities

   This is a box that contains all the items that you will need as soon as you move into the new place. You must have one such box to prevent you from randomly opening different boxes to find things you need. Things like toiletries, hammers, nails, and a box cutter should be present in this box.

10. Organizing Boxes

    Decluttering while preparing for a move involves packing boxes in preparation for the day you move. As you declutter and fill up different boxes, ensure you are putting labels on them while using tape to seal the box shut. Move the box to out of the room to create space to continue decluttering.

    Choose an empty room or free space in the home where you can start stacking the boxes as you bring them out. The label on each box should indicate what room it is going to. You should also inscribe a list of the items in the box.

Quick Action Step

It is easy to read a book and forget about it once you learn and adopt the various principles given in the book. For this chapter, it is easy to overlook since it may not currently apply to your situation. To ensure you can find this chapter when it becomes necessary, create a note that refers you back to this book when you need to prepare for a move.

Conclusion

Clutter consists of anything that you can quickly identify as trash in the home. Understanding that other regular items in the house identify as clutter is the reason you can conclude that you have a clutter problem in the home. A clutter problem has a significant impact both physically and mentally making it vital that you eliminate clutter in your home.

Decluttering is the process you adopt to rid your home of clutter effectively. It is a process that can take a bit of time but is well worth it in the end. Decluttering is not something you jump into. It requires a lot of changes in your life. First, you have to develop a mindset to properly implement this process while also developing the discipline to ensure that you can keep up with the demands of the process.

If you are feeling down and incompetent just because your home is filled with clutter, you are far from the truth. According to various stats on clutter, a significant percentage of homes around the world face a similar problem. Although it can be attributed to the consumerist lifestyle, you must focus more on the solution rather than beating yourself up.

The different chapters in this book have given an insight into some of the vital aspects of decluttering that you would benefit beneficial to your home decluttering efforts. From the importance of focusing on small wins, you find out about how this strategy can help you overcome the feeling of being overwhelmed anytime you face the clutter in your home. It also extends to the importance of donating some of your items and where these items will be better appreciated.

The idea of focusing on small wins is very significant when considering how to declutter each room in the home. Certain rooms are much more comfortable to declutter than others, and you learn the reason for this as you read through. Areas like the kitchen, bathroom, laundry room, garage, attic, and basement are spaces that require the divide and conquer approach to decluttering. In these areas, the clutter you need to declutter often requires additional time compared to other areas of the home.

This book promised to provide a step-by-step guide on how to declutter the home. Since decluttering is a process that you don't just jump into, you need to create a plan on how to go about it. By offering key steps that are effective in decluttering specific rooms in the home, you have the upper hand in ridding the home of clutter.

A particular chapter dedicated to decluttering sentimental items offers an in-depth look at the solution to one of the most significant problems individuals face during the decluttering process. Some tips can help you get over the emotions associated with sentimental items, as well as excellent ways on how to keep the memories attached to these items alive without having to depend on their physical presence.

If there is anything that you must take away

from this book, then you must understand the importance of small wins. Your focus on small wins is an approach to clutter problems that you can use, as well as for your other life endeavors. Through this approach, you learn that when tackling a problem that seems overwhelming, all you need to do is break it down into smaller parts that are easier to handle.

After completing a small part of the task, you celebrate your small win to gain motivation to move on to the next task. Repeating this process will get you to the finish line in a more straightforward manner than if you attempt to go big on the first try. If there is one thing you should take home from this book, it's that with consistent effort you can have a beautiful de-cluttered home to enjoy!

References

35 Surprising Home Organization Statistics That'll Inspire You to Tidy Up. (2019). Retrieved from https://www.organizedinteriors.com/blog/home-organization-statistics/

Babauta, L. (2013). Declutter Your Life : zen habits. Retrieved from https://zenhabits.net/declutter/

Browne, K. (2019). Strategies to Let Go of Sentimental Items. Retrieved from https://www.getorganizedwizard.com/blog/2019/03/strategies-to-let-go-of-sentimental-items/

Ewer, C. (2019). Declutter 101: Strategies To Cut Clutter | Organized Home. Retrieved from https://organizedhome.com/cut-clutter/declutter-101-strategies-cut-clutter

How To Declutter Your Books - Tale Away. (2019). Retrieved from http://taleaway.com/how-to-declutter-your-books/

How to Declutter Your Home in One Day. (2018). Retrieved from https://www.showmesuburban.com/how-to-declutter-your-house-in-one-day/

How to Declutter Your Home: A Ridiculously Thorough Guide | Budget Dumpster. (2019). Retrieved from https://www.budgetdumpster.com/resources/how-to-declutter-your-home.php#garage

Hudson, K. (2019). What are small wins?. Retrieved from http://smallwinsinnovation.com/small-wins/

Jones, R. (2017). Tips to Declutter Your Home Before a Move - Nourishing Minimalism. Retrieved from https://nourishingminimalism.com/blog/declutter-your-home-before-move/

Larkin, E. (2019). A Foolproof Method for Decluttering Your Home. Retrieved from https://www.thespruce.com/decluttering-your-entire-home-2648002

Lawson, A. (2019). Organizing Books with the

KonMari Method. Retrieved from https://justagirlandherblog.com/the-konmari-method-organizing-books/

Rodgers, H. (2013). Day 21: Fridge {31 Days of Easy Decluttering}. Retrieved from http://www.fromoverwhelmedtoorganizedblog.com/2013/10/day-21-fridge-31-days-of-easy.html

Rodgers, H. (2013). Day 13: Pantry {31 Days of Easy Decluttering}. Retrieved from http://www.fromoverwhelmedtoorganizedblog.com/2013/10/day-13-pantry-31-days-of-easy.html

Russell, M. (2019). How to Declutter your Storage Room without Feeling Overwhelmed - Simple Lionheart Life. Retrieved from https://simplelionheartlife.com/declutter-your-storage-room/

Stillman, J. (2015). 5 Steps to Get the Right Mindset for Success. Retrieved from https://www.inc.com/jessica-stillman/5-steps-to-get-the-right-mindset-for-success.html

Yang, S. (2016). https://www.realsimple.com.

Retrieved from https://www.realsimple.com/home-organizing/organizing/declutter-garage